The Legitimacy of the Business Corporation
in the Law of the United States, 1780–1970

The Legitimacy
of the
Business Corporation
in the
Law of the United States
1780–1970

James Willard Hurst

The University Press of Virginia
Charlottesville

THE UNIVERSITY PRESS OF VIRGINIA
Copyright © 1970 by the Rector and Visitors
of the University of Virginia

First published 1970

Standard Book Number: 8139-0291-6
Library of Congress Catalog Card Number: 79-110750
Printed in the United States of America

Acknowledgments

I AM grateful to the University of Virginia for the invitation to deliver the Page-Barbour Lectures of 1969, from which these essays derive. My appreciation goes also to Dean Monrad Paulsen and Professor Neill Alford, Jr., and their colleagues of Virginia's law faculty for providing a most hospitable setting for the lectures.

The hypotheses which the essays develop have grown out of a long-term program of work seeking to relate the history of law to the general history of the United States. Over some years I have been indebted for support in this effort to the Social Science Research Council, the Rockefeller Foundation, the administration of the University of Wisconsin, and the trustees of the William F. Vilas Trust Estate, under whose auspices I hold a chair as Vilas Professor of Law in the University of Wisconsin. Of course, the essays do not purport to speak for any of these agencies, and I take sole responsibility for what I write.

JAMES WILLARD HURST

Madison, Wisconsin
June 25, 1969

Contents

Analytical Table of Contents

The Legitimacy of the Business Corporation
in the Law of the United States, 1780–1970

Introduction

Time, Place, and Subject

T HESE essays deal with the growth of public policy concerning the business corporation in the United States. The first two essays deal with the substance of policy in two periods which show distinctive patterns: from about 1780 to the 1880's and from about 1890 into the 1960's. The third examines the contributions to this history by the major agencies through which lawmakers determine policy.

In the second half of the twentieth century the business corporation—especially the very large corporation—plays leading roles of bewildering diversity on a world stage, and not only in the United States. These essays deal only with a modest, though important sector, of policy about the business corporation. It provides perspective to take preliminary note of two boundaries of the discussion. First, we deal with policy which is almost wholly a homegrown, North American product. This concentration is realistic. Our practice and policy concerning the business corporation grew out of our own experience; in this area of life we did not borrow much from anyone else. Second, these essays focus on the law most immediately relevant to corporate organization and behavior and not upon aspects of business corporations which primarily concern the sociologist, economist, and political scientist. There are good reasons for specialized attention to the law of corporations. But realism calls for caution that from this emphasis we not exaggerate law's contribution to the sum of corporate business.

Both in the colonial years and after independence, corporation law was a homemade product. This was true even of the central doctrine which insisted that the sovereign's action was required to create a corporation.

The law of republican and imperial Rome dealt with public

and private corporate bodies. Later the medieval church developed doctrine concerning ecclesiastical associations. To maintain central authority over diverse potential competitors, the Roman state and the church at times found it expedient to declare that legally effective corporate being required an act of the civil or religious sovereign—or at least a license. Scholars would find here analogies in idea and practice to later developments in England and the United States. Yet what the church did had no direct bearing on profit-seeking enterprise, and at some stages Roman law seems to have treated as legal entities business associations formed wholly by private action. Thus, analogy is all we find.[1]

English law on corporations responded to English experience. There is little indication that English policy makers followed, or even knew much, Roman doctrine. Religious bodies were formed in England with papal sanction. But what churchmen did in their own establishments seems not to have materially influenced ideas or action about secular organization; at most the church's doctrine figured in secular policy when spokesmen for Crown authority borrowed it for their own partisan arguments.[2] In England long before men accepted the need for, or sought, a creative act of King or Parliament, they organized boroughs for defense and guilds for trade, and in so doing built functioning entities out of experience rather than with official license. Official license first became important when boroughs or trade guilds sought special privileges from national lawmakers. But such grants did not create legal entities; they bestowed particular privileges on entities already existing in fact and accepted by law as legitimate.[3] However, in the Tudor period boroughs and

---

[1] On Roman law: Berle (1), 3, 4: Timberg, 554, 555: Williston, 107; *cf.* Livermore, 11, note 4, and 12, note 4. On canon law: Dodd (2), 981; Livermore, 11, note 4; Stevens (1), 333; Timberg, 540. Ecclesiastical associations and the doctrine that they owed their existence to official acts of creation existed through the Middle Ages alongside business associations, which did not purport to exist by official license. Berle (1), 5.

[2] Berle (1), 7, 8; Livermore, 10 and 11, note 4.

[3] Berle (1), 7, 8; Plumb, 36, 37, 42; Livermore, 16, 17. Later doctrine paid implicit tribute to the fact that many municipal and philanthropic corporations grew out of practice rather than by royal charter, when such bodies were said sometimes to exist by prescription, out of long

guilds commonly obtained royal charters declaring their entity character. There were diverse factors behind this new emphasis on chartering. Charters were in part a *quid pro quo* for special privileges which only the increasingly powerful national government could provide. In part charters borrowed for the chartered units some of the prestige and legitimacy of this new central authority. The major impetus derived from the need of the national authority to assert itself and to establish its superiority in law over otherwise divisive local governments or interest groups.[4] By 1628 Coke could assert firmly that royal authorization was necessary to create a corporation. The claim was not then contested, though after the Restoration the Stuarts characteristically pressed the matter into controversy by seeking to change charter rights of boroughs and thereby contributed to the advent of William and Mary. Yet in the outcome the Revolution of 1688 continued the basic theme. By the eighteenth century the accepted English doctrine was that only the king in Parliament might create a corporation.[5]

The prime purposes which encouraged the growth of this English policy were political and not economic. The impelling objective was to help focus and secure political power at the head of the state. Values of governmental or business efficiency might move the grantees of charters. But through the early seventeenth century these were not the prime concerns of the Crown, which took the lead in asserting the national government's exclusive creative authority.[6] However, the corporate device did in fact have great functional possibilities for helping business enterprise. The English experience showed that the inherent tension between the political and the economic relevance of the corporation tended to bring the economic aspect to the fore when concern for the political dimension was less sharply felt.

---

reliance on presumed lost charters. Livermore, 10 and 11, note 4; Williston, 114.

[4] Berle (1), 7; Livermore, 10 and 11, note 4, 13, note 9, 15, 18, 243; Joseph H. Smith, 664; Stevens (1), 333.

[5] Berle (1) 9, 11, 15; Dodd (2), 981, 982; Livermore, 18; Plumb, 53–60; Timberg, 554.

[6] See note 5, *supra*.

This interplay became apparent in the seventeenth-century development of the law concerning foreign trading corporations. From the late sixteenth century royal chartering of companies to develop foreign trade and colonies was a prominent feature of national policy. A royal charter was essential to such ventures. In times of political uncertainty merchants who combined for a foreign venture without explicit royal sanction risked prosecution for criminal conspiracy against the national interest. Moreover, the royal charter legitimized a range of public functions performed by such trading companies in organizing terms of trade, setting up local governments, controlling customs, and, in effect, making foreign policy in their areas of operation. Thus in this early phase such corporate privileges as served private profit seeking were an incidental return for the public jobs the corporation undertook. But throughout the late seventeenth century trade began to bulk larger than public functions in the activities of such companies. By the eighteenth century English lawmakers and businessmen alike had come to regard the corporation mainly as a structure useful to private trading operations; public responsibilities receded so far into the background as to become of secondary account. A parallel development in common law highlighted this emphasis on the private utilities of such corporations: judges ruled that charters should be deemed to give trade monopolies only against other chartered companies and that unincorporated traders might lawfully compete at will with such trading companies.[7] The shift in English policy from a focus upon political considerations to a focus upon economic utility anticipated a much later analogous course of policy in the United States. The shift in focus was not without a good deal of blurring of policy. Because the policy context of the corporation before the eighteenth century was primarily one of political concerns, the new emphasis—when men began to value the corporation mainly for its business utility—represented different goals and presented different tensions of interest from those that had determined prior attitudes toward corporate organization. The earlier political context influenced policy in the business-corpo-

[7] Cooke, 52, 54, 58, 61, 62, 65; Goebel, x, xiii; Stevens (1), 2, 101, 102; Williston, 114.

ration period that followed, but it did so largely by confusing issues. The earlier tradition helped generate a diffuse distrust of the corporate form and—a closely related effect—impeded perception of the distinction between issues of power and of utility.[8] In this aspect, also, the English experience anticipated, though it did not produce, the later course of events in the United States.

Other aspects of English law reflected developing pressures to legitimize continuing relationships of economic utility. The strong assertion that men might enjoy corporate status only by royal charter or act of Parliament never excluded other legally sanctioned forms of association. The law of contract, becoming broad in scope and flexible, encouraged men to devise agreements to manage assets. Thus the common law early and consistently recognized binding relations of principal and agent, between themselves as well as to third parties. Under common law men might effectively commit themselves as joint venturers for a particular voyage or for particular transactions. The eighteenth and early nineteenth centuries saw elaboration of the law of partnership to support business associations of more continuity. Since the fifteenth century Equity had vigorously developed the trust; this was not typically a device of business, but it provided an enduring relationship for administering assets.[9]

Developments most relevant to the business corporation derived from the Bubble Act of 1719. Designed to favor powerful chartered interests—and also in reaction to speculative excesses connnected with unincorporated financial firms of the prior decade—this act of Parliament declared unlawful the operation of unincorporated joint stock companies with transferable shares. The statute did not outlaw corporations. But its enactment showed a general distrust of, and discouraged applications for, statutory charters, especially since this disenchantment also found expression in a tendency to insist that charters impose on shareholders liability for a company's debts. However, the Bubble Act was drawn in vague terms, simply forbidding men to act as a corporation without a charter; unless an association em-

8 *Cf.* Berle (1), 11, 15; Gower (1), 536.
9 Dodd (2), 986 ff.; Radin, 152, 154.

ployed corporate formalities, such as a common seal, it was quite uncertain what constituted acting as a corporation. Meanwhile the growth of business pressed men to seek the advantages of pooling capital and effort. Responsive to these utilitarian demands and adapting the trust device, courts of Equity in the eighteenth century accepted the legitimacy of pooling assets by a deed of settlement, which put the pooled resources in the control of trustees to manage them for designated business purposes. Equity would recognize the transferability of shares in such a pool. By the early nineteenth century such an arrangement might even include limited liability for debts; creditors had notice by virtue of the designation of the operation as a "limited" company. Parliament's repeal of the Bubble Act in 1825 remitted to the common law the legal status of unincorporated business associations. Shortly before the repeal, a dictum of Lord Eldon declared it a common law offense for an unchartered group to act as a corporation. But there seems to be no recorded common law criminal proceeding of such character. And, in any event, to act under a deed of settlement was not to act as a corporation. The perfected technique of the business association organized under a deed of settlement deprived of practical significance both Eldon's dictum and the prohibition of the Bubble Act. Moreover, use of the deed-of-settlement technique accustomed businessmen and lawyers alike to the idea that men should enjoy considerable contractual freedom in arranging business associations. This approach was thus the more readily carried into the English Companies Acts of 1844 and 1855, statutes that made incorporation generally available.[10] Again, English experience anticipated, though it did not affect, developments in United States policy. Beginning in the late nineteenth century policy here increasingly showed a similar readiness to accord broad contract freedom to organizers of business corporations. Common to such legal developments in both England and the United States was an undercurrent in favor of ar-

[10] Cooke, 86–88, 96, 99, 100 and 100, note 1, 105, 109, 123, 124, 128; Gower (2), 1370, 1371, 1376, 1378; Livermore, 62; Manne (1), 429, note 95 x.

rangements that fostered economic promotion over other economic and political considerations.

All of these developments in England were products of English experience, minimally affected, if at all, by borrowings from civil or canon law. Likewise, corporation law developed in this country in the colonial years and after independence out of North American experience, with scant borrowing from, or even knowledge of, English law. A basic factor from 1608 into the second half of the eighteenth century was the simple condition of the economy along the North Atlantic coast. There is no evidence of significant demand for corporate charters for local enterprise until about 1780; both opportunity and means were lacking for undertakings ambitious enough to invite using the corporation.

Thus for over 150 years after settlement began in English North America there was no need to pay attention to the growth of English corporation law. Even in the mother country public policy had as yet drawn little distinction between governmental, eleemosynary, and business corporations; the first English treatise on corporations (Kyd 1794) has little to say, and scant authority to cite, concerning use of the corporation for economic enterprise. Hence, it is not surprising that to the end of the eighteenth century in the United States law had developed no separate policy or rules on business corporations; the same legislative committees handled applications for all types of corporate charters, and when questions arose, courts applied to business corporations the judge-made law that had developed out of problems of ecclesiastical, philanthropic, and municipal corporations.[11]

Of course, English chartered companies were prominent in establishing North Atlantic colonies. But with time the political functions were increasingly differentiated from the economic functions of such charters until the charters had significance solely as political constitutions; also corporate trading early and

[11] Angell and Ames, v, vi; Davis, 2:4, 316; Dodd (8), 255, 256, and (23), 1, 6, 195–98; Williston, 105. *Cf.* Kyd, 1:28–29, 258, 261, 262, 272, 273–75, 292, 299, 300, 302, 2:311.

rapidly gave way to the business initiative of individuals, joint venturers, and partners. This course of events ran counter to that of the Great East India Company, in whose career the trading element tended to gain at the expense of the political.[12] In North America the dominant and growing population was English derived; in contrast, in the Indies Englishmen were a small minority in a sea of native inhabitants of different culture. The social origins of the North American settlers and the combination of economic opportunity and rude setting fostered growth through dispersion of individual energy rather than through concentrated organization. Potentially the most direct link between North America and English policy regarding the business corporation was the 1741 act of Parliament that extended the Bubble Act to the colonies. Conceivably this statute may have clouded the legitimacy of unincorporated associations enough to discourage their formation. But the act was never invoked to attack an unincorporated joint stock company, though several of these appeared in the colonies, and there is no evidence that the statute had effect. This want of general impact fits the background of the act. The 1741 statute extended the Bubble Act in specific response to objections to a Boston merchant's project to organize a bank which would issue bills of credit to members on the security of real estate. Thus, despite its broad terms, the 1741 act sprang from concern only with the particular problem of note-issuing banks; a similar concern was to be the focus of most general attacks against corporations in the first half of the nineteenth century.[13]

In sum, when we began making important use of the corporation for business in the United States from about 1780, there was little relevant legal experience on which to draw. For 100 years, we proceeded to use the corporate instrument on a scale unmatched in England. In that development we built public policy toward the corporation almost wholly out of our own wants and concerns, shaped primarily by our own institutions. The one definite inheritance was the idea that some positive act of

[12] Cooke, 54, 58, 61, 62; *cf.* Livermore, 215.

[13] Davis, 1:5, especially 428, 439; Goebel, xxii, xxiii; Hammond, 24–25, 28.

the sovereign was necessary to create corporate status. But we gave our own content to that idea.

This historic emphasis on the law's creative act invites the second comment preliminary to the essays that follow. Law and law-oriented thinking have been so woven into use of the corporate instrument that we need caution against exaggerating the importance of the legal components in what has been a complex development.

The standard formula spoke as if the state not only gave an indispensable consent but itself created the whole working reality of any business association which took corporate form. Borrowing from Coke and Blackstone, Marshall gave this view classic expression in his opinion for the Court in the *Dartmouth College* case (1819): "A corporation is an artificial being, invisible, intangible, and existing only in contemplation of law. Being the mere creature of law, it possesses only those properties which the charter of its creation confers upon it, either expressly, or as incidental to its very existence." [14] About 100 years later, when the corporation had become the dominant type of business organization, others estimated the law's role as no less critical. However, these commentators emphasized less the law's formal license than particular operating privileges it conferred. In the early twentieth century Harvard's Charles W. Eliot regarded stockholders' limited liability as "the corporation's most precious characteristic," and "by far the most effective legal invention . . . made in the nineteenth century." Columbia's Nicholas Murray Butler was ponderously confident: "I weigh my words when I say that in my judgment the limited liability corporation is the greatest single discovery of modern times. . . . Even steam and electricity are far less important than the limited liability corporation, and they would be reduced to comparative impotence without it." [15] In contrast, appraising the matter in 1960, Professor Bayless Manning radically downgraded the significance of corporation law as a force shaping our history. The nineteenth-century legal mind had pur-

[14] The Trustees of Dartmouth College v. Woodward, 4 Wheaton 518, 636 (U.S. 1819).
[15] Cataldo, 473.

sued a phantom. It "vividly saw the 'corporation'—the legal construct—as something quite separate from the economic enterprise, three dimensional, virtually alone, a little bit sacred because of its 'immortality' and connection with the 'sovereign,' and withal terribly important." In the mid-twentieth century Manning felt that "the commercial image of the business organization has emerged to overshadow the concept of the 'corporation.'" In consequence, "corporation law, as a field of intellectual effort, is dead in the United States. When American law ceased to take the 'corporation' seriously, the entire body of law that had been built upon that intellectual construct slowly perforated and rotted away. We have nothing left but our great empty corporation statutes—towering skyscrapers of rusted girders, internally welded together and containing nothing but wind." [16]

If we must strike a net balance, Manning seems somewhat closer to reality. Corporation law has always been an instrument of wants and energies derived from sources outside the law; it has not been a prime mover. However, means can materially affect the content of ends to which they are put, and the kind of tools men can obtain may decide the jobs they can do. Marshall, Butler, and Eliot distort reality if they locate in the law the springs of action—the deeper sources of ambition and purpose—behind the use of the corporation. They grasp reality insofar as they mean only that the kind of structure, procedures, and privileges which corporation law made available significantly channeled the expression of men's wants and energies and significantly affected the responses which other interests made to these drives. Manning's tart skepticism corrects metaphysical and vainglorious exaggeration of the importance of the sovereign's gift of legal entity to business associations. But his vivid metaphors do not give proper weight to more workaday aspects of the historic record—the effects of the corporation both as an instrument alone and as an instrument whose utilities created significant social value issues.

From 1780 on it was businessmen who created business firms and determined whether firms died or lived, passed quickly or

16 Manning (3), 245, and 245, note 37.

took an institutional character. It was businessmen who developed the goals, organization, and procedures of corporations. As business developed its organizational skills and learned how to muster and discipline large and complex resources of capital and manpower, business corporations developed their own kinds of social structure and internal politics.[17] Moreover, from 1780 on the corporation was often used to organize operations which affected, or were seen as affecting, political power, social class, and the relative or competitive growth of different sectors of the total economy or different geographical areas. Thus from the start corporate enterprise was often in fact, or in any case was seen as being, a distinct social and political as well as an economic factor in the general life.[18] For all these reasons, though these essays center on the law pertaining to the corporation, they of necessity recognize that this legal history exists in a social context.

However, it is realistic also to give special attention to the law of corporate enterprise. Since 1780 the use of the corporation in business has been treated as presenting important questions of public policy to be resolved through legal processes. That concern expressed itself in one of the earliest, most continuous streams of statute lawmaking in our history, in a great bulk of judge-made law (both apart from, and based on, legislation and constitutions), and—in the twentieth century—in significant bodies of federal and state administrative law. In this flow of policy making lawyers have been much involved with businessmen in giving character to corporate enterprise—as draftsmen, counselors, lobbyists, advocates, and public officials. We must not exaggerate the influence of men of law compared with the inventions and energies of promoters, financiers, managers, marketing men, trade union leaders, and a host of others. In the whole course of affairs lawyers produced only marginal effect. But the law provided leverage at points critical to other development, and its marginal effects could determine the bal-

[17] Cochran (1) 8–15, 219–28; Drucker (4), 3–4, 8–15; Moore, 4–10, 192–96.

[18] Bruchey, 128–33; Eells (1), 20, 29, 47–49, 77–94; Whyte, 4–10, 17–22, 31, 43–45, 49–59.

ance finally struck among a complex of other factors at work to fix our direction and the pace at which we moved. The whole story is one of intricate detail, beyond what these essays can encompass. What the essays attempt to do is to identify some main trends and organizing themes within which the detailed development proceeded.

Chapter I

From Special Privilege to General Utility
1780–1890

FROM the 1780's into the 1880's the course of public policy reflected tensions among three different social evaluations of the business corporation. The various approaches included practical acceptance, principled rejection, and explicit general license. If this array of attitudes suggests muddle, there was indeed muddle, at its murkiest about mid-century. In retrospect, however, we can see (1) from 1780 into the 1820's a period in which policy was being shaped by legislative practice, (2) from about 1830 to 1870 a time of considerable confusion between practice and talk, and (3) in the 1870's and 1880's the achievement of what appeared to be an equilibrium in which earlier particularized practice took on declared general form. The 1880's resolution proved short-lived in the face of strong currents of change in the economy. Between about 1890 and 1930 we created a new frame of policy within which we gave businessmen a free hand in adapting the corporate instrument to their will. From the 1930's through the 1960's we continued to accept this freedom in the private design of corporate organization. At the same time we showed disquiet at the growth of the practical power and impact of big corporations by creating *ad hoc* a new body of regulatory law mainly relevant to the activities of large-scale corporate enterprise. Thus the record falls into two rather discrete chapters of policy growth—one rounded out between 1780 and the late 1880's and the other running from about 1890 into the 1960's. In the second chapter a clear-cut pattern had yet to emerge as of 1970.

The confusion between practice and debate which swirled for a generation starting about 1830 flowed out of the first decades of substantial use of the corporation for business after 1780. The years from 1780 into the 1820's showed that legislative practice may become sufficiently patterned to constitute a policy and also sufficiently diversified to breed quarrels out of obscurity if the diversity is unacknowledged.

Of course, in the simple late-eighteenth-century economy most business went on merely by private contract; the law never required that all business associations be chartered by the state. The rapid elaboration of the law of partnership by the early nineteenth century undoubtedly reflected the long-standing popularity of that style of unincorporated enterprise. Promoters formed unincorporated joint stock associations to market lands, and for these they devised terms of organization familiar in corporations.[1] However, even in the colonial years royal governors and colonial legislatures chartered some business corporations. After independence the desire of businessmen to use the corporation mounted rapidly; state legislatures chartered 317 business corporations from 1780 to 1801.[2] We lack evidence to compare the use of the corporation with the resort to its nearest informal analogue, the unincorporated joint stock company. But there is no solid evidence that such unincorporated ventures set the norm for associated enterprise or that corporate charters merely copied what private contract had thus already accomplished. Given a simple economy, the inference is rather that these 317 corporate charters represented the main type of the most ambitious and sophisticated business associations of the time. This inference fits the later record, which shows no broad use of the unincorporated joint-stock company.[3] By 1830 the trend was plain: the corporation would emerge as the preferred style of structured business organization.

Parallelling businessmen's desire for the corporation in the late eighteenth century was a steady implicit adherence to the idea that only a positive act of the sovereign might create corporate status. We were familiar with this idea from our colonial beginnings. Trading companies which founded colonies existed

---

[1] Bruchey, 139–40; Dodd (8), 255–56; Handlin, 131–32; Livermore, 215–22.

[2] Davis, 2:27, table 111.

[3] Dodd (8), 260, 261, and (11), 358; Hurst (4), 409; *cf.* Livermore, 295, 297.

under royal charters. In fact, the charters proved more relevant to political organization than to trade. But this development itself heightened the notion that incorporation had a peculiarly close tie to the sovereign. Such corporations as local initiative promoted in the colonies all claimed legitimacy by grants from colonial governors or legislatures. After independence the consistent practice was to create corporations by special statute. True, in England there were boroughs and trade guilds which had come into being and acted as corporate bodies out of the cumulated practice of local groups; English lawmakers later rationalized the legitimacy of these bodies as being based on prescription derived from "lost" royal charters. The shorter, simpler life of the North American colonies gave no scope for such a development; colonial law did not include the idea of corporate status achieved by prescription or usage. Knowing their Coke and Blackstone, lawmen in the United States could thus readily accept the established seventeenth-century English doctrine that only the sovereign's act might make a corporation. Moreover almost all of the business enterprises incorporated here in the formative generation starting in the 1780's were chartered for activities of some community interest—supplying transport, water, insurance, or banking facilities. That such public-interest undertakings practically monopolized the corporate form implied that incorporation was inherently of such public concern that the public authority must confer it. Against this background legislators, courts, and law writers in the early nineteenth century undertook to make more explicit statements of public policy toward the corporation and confidently asserted that men could have corporate status in law only by grant from the legislature.[4]

Two aspects of our practice fostered the idea not only that the legislature's grant was necessary to incorporation but that it authoritatively fixed the scope and content of corporate organization. A statutory charter usually had content beyond a

[4] For 1780–1800: Berle (1), 17, and (10), 946, note 2; Brandeis (1), 548; Cooke, 62; Dodd (2), 984; Handlin, 151. For 1800–1850: Angell and Ames, v, 38, 59; Cadman, 8, 9, 94–101; Dodd (10), 6, 7, and (23), 151, 154; Hartz (1), 82; Henderson, 6, 7, 21, 34, 35.

mere license for private will; in its details it was more like a constitution, fixing the internal structure of the corporation. The consistent practice of creating corporations by special statute promoted this attitude. A statute was among the most formal acts of state and claimed force from its enactment and not from anything private persons did before or after it was put on the books. Incorporation by special statute thus launched our corporations in an official frame of reference, in contrast to the emphasis on private agreement and invention in the contemporary English development of joint stock companies created under deeds of settlement.[5] A second element worked to similar effect. In the late eighteenth century the states were liberally chartering religious and philanthropic associations along with economic enterprises. This liberality produced enactment of general incorporation laws for nonprofit bodies long before such statutes were acceptable for business ventures. Such religious or welfare institutions existed to serve indefinite constituencies; in contrast the interests of the enrolled stockholders provided the legitimating goals for business corporations. Benevolent donors might launch churches, schools, or hospitals, but typically they fulfilled their function in the act of giving and provided no continuing surveillance of the institutions. Thus we were early accustomed to find the legitimacy and authority of an important type of corporation only in the laws which sanctioned them.[6] The practice of chartering business firms by special statute and the multiplication of religious and welfare corporations continued as the main currents of the law's dealings with the corporate device into the mid-nineteenth century. Thus a long span of years habituated us to thinking not only that the law alone might create a corporation, but also that only the creating law gave the corporation its effective content. Marshall's opinion for the Court in the *Dartmouth College* case attested and strengthened this attitude. That decision extended the protection of the contract clause of the Federal Constitution not only over a donor's gift and the college's existing assets but also over the frame of organization and powers of the institution

[5] Cooke, 86, 87; Gower (2), 1372, 1376.
[6] Brandeis (1), 548; Latty (1), 25, note 42.

as created by the original charter, as against later intruding legislation. What the corporate charter gave and what the Constitution protected was thus not only an official license but also a pattern for organizing certain human relations.[7]

Our policy thus rested on the proposition that corporate status might exist only by the sovereign's grant or concession. Practice moved toward the corollary—though it was not a necessary one—that the whole of the corporation's structure and powers must be found in the terms of the sovereign's concession. These propositions seemed to present a straightforward policy. But overlapping and running past this apparently simple trend was another continuity of practice which implied values and tensions less simple and inviting controversy.

From the 1780's well into mid-nineteenth century the most frequent and conspicuous use of the business corporation—especially under special charters—was for one particular type of enterprise, that which we later called public utility and put under particular regulation because of its special impact in the community. Tallies of special charters for this period are strikingly similar over time and place. Of the 317 separate-enterprise special charters enacted from 1780 to 1801 in the states, nearly two-thirds were for enterprises concerned with transport (inland navigation, turnpikes, toll bridges); another 20 per cent were for banks or insurance companies; 10 per cent were for the provision of local public services (mostly water supply); less than 4 per cent were for general business corporations. Counts for two of the older state economies show like patterns. Of 2,318 special charters enacted in New Jersey from 1791 to 1875, about a third were for transport, 16 per cent for financial companies, and 6 per cent for local utilities; about 42 per cent were for manufacturing and other general business enterprises. Of 2,333 special charters enacted in Pennsylvania from 1790 to 1860, 64 per cent were for transport enterprises, 18 per cent for financial companies, and 6 per cent for local utilities; manufacturing and other general business firms accounted for only about

[7] The Trustees of Dartmouth College v. Woodward, 4 Wheaton 518 (U.S. 1819); Dodd (1), 595, 596, (2), 985, and (23), 27, 28; James B. Robbins, 165.

8 per cent. In a younger state, developing in a later span of years, the emphasis shifts, but there is still a resemblance to the older patterns. Of 1,130 special charters enacted in Wisconsin from 1848 to 1871, 38 per cent were for transportation companies, 10 per cent for financial companies, and 4 per cent for local utilities; on the other hand, 42 per cent of these Wisconsin charters were for manufacturing, mining, and lumber firms. Over-all, until the 1830's the special-charter era was marked by the striking predominance of incorporation for enterprises which provided framework or base facilities for other economic activity and which furnished services on which their customers were peculiarly dependent. From the 1830's this pattern was qualified by the rather rapid relative increase in charters for a general range of business, especially for manufacturing. Thus in New Jersey chartered enterprise consisted almost exclusively of transportation companies in the 1790's, and they continued dominant through 1820; but manufacturing and mining—so outnumbered before 1820—accounted for over 32 per cent of all New Jersey charters enacted between 1820 and 1844, and in those years comparative figures on capitalization also reflect a relatively large rise in manufacturing companies. As the nineteenth century progressed, wider use of machinery probably gave impetus to incorporation of a relatively increasing number of industrial concerns. So even in Wisconsin's simple economy, industrial charters began to overtake public-utility-type charters between 1848 and 1871. Increasing familiarity with the corporation as an instrument of an extending range of ordinary business contributed in the seventies and eighties to abandonment of special charters in favor of legislation which made incorporation generously available under simple procedures for practically any lawful enterprise.[8]

We should not use hindsight to translate known outcomes into purposes or perceptions not held by the actors. But we may properly use hindsight to see better what results, what operating trends, and what gains and costs were building over time,

[8] Davis, 2:27, table III (1780–1801); Cadman, 206, 207, tables I, II, and 211 (New Jersey); Hartz (1), 38, and Miller, 150 (Pennsylvania); Kuehnl, 143, table V (Wisconsin).

whether or not contemporaries saw them. So from our perspective we can see that several different legal products and policies were involved in the broad flow of legislation in which corporate charters figured so largely from the 1780's into mid-nineteenth century.

1. There were rights, duties, privileges, and immunities which men might enjoy in business association, or which might be imposed on them, only according to terms affirmatively defined by law and not merely by private agreement. Though contemporaries often did not make a distinction, two kinds of such uniquely law-made incidents were involved in the growth of public policy toward the business corporation.

a) There were some elements of corporate business organization which law recognized only on terms which it affirmatively defined; so far as these law-made factors figured, it could truly be said that the positive action of lawmakers was essential to confer corporate status. Such were the capacities of men in association to act as a single entity in law—to sue and be sued, to hold and transfer title to real or personal property, to act with legal effect under a common seal. Such was the capacity of an enterprise to continue undisturbed in law by change in shareholders, whether involuntary (as by death) or voluntary (as by sale of interests). Such was a law-given immunity of shareholders from liability for claims of third parties against the enterprise, whether or not third parties had notice or assented, or whether they claimed in contract or in tort. These were all elements which gave a business association legally recognized character as a separate entity. As legal doctrine and lawyers' and businessmen's ingenuity developed over the years, incorporation was not the only means of securing some of these elements. However, only corporate status conferred assured immunity of investors for debts of an enterprise; only corporate status offered a ready means of obtaining group capacity to sue or be sued as one; and, in fact, from the early nineteenth century on the corporation became the most sought-after and economically influential device for obtaining the general pattern of entity features. In any case, insofar as entity characteristics could be obtained without incorporation, lawmakers still set the terms to a material degree—in the judge-made law of trusts and in statute law (mainly of the twentieth century) bestowing entity characteristics on limited partnerships and joint stock companies. To operate with legal effect as an entity was a quality of business association determined by law.[9]

b) There were other capacities which law alone could confer, which performed the function not of creating a legal entity but of allowing the grantees to use assets or exact payments or impose burdens on others in ways which would have been either impracticable or illegal or both without the law's specific sanction. Such were franchises permitting the grantees to act in ways not open to the general run of men: to establish a turnpike, canal, or railroad right of way; to fix tolls, within a broad range of discretion, for use of facilities (notably transport facilities) on which the users were much dependent; to issue promises to pay (bank notes), which the law would permit to circulate as a medium of exchange; to exercise the state's power of eminent domain; to enjoy an implicit, if not explicit, monopoly of some profitable field of enterprise (as when the legislature granted only a limited number of railroad or bank charters in a given locality); to erect dams for power or navigation improvement or other works which without a statutory franchise would be open to legal attack as a public or private nuisance. Legislatures gave some of these franchises in great numbers to individuals and to unincorporated groups, especially for power dams and navigation improvements. However, most of these special-action franchises were in fact given to corporations. Usually there was no explicit declaration that only corporations might lawfully receive such franchises, though by the mid-nineteenth century statutes commonly limited the issue of bank notes to incorporated banks.[10]

2. There were many elements of business organization which men might lawfully arrange among themselves by private agree-

[9] Dodd (2), 986–88, 991–92, 996, and (7), 29; Evans, 10, 21, 64; Hornstein (4), 1:12, 15–17, 20; Stevens (1), 14–23.

[10] Cadman, 91, 189, 194; Handlin, 107, 108, 112, 207; Hartz (1), 70, 72, 76; Henderson, 68–69; Hurst (4) 143–44, 175–204, 273–78; Livermore, 245, 248; Stevens (1), 6.

ment within the broad scope offered by the general law of contract. By private agreement, co-venturers might define their respective shares in an enterprise, distribute authority among themselves (as between contributors of capital and managers), and even arrange immunity of shareholders for enterprise debts, in contrast to third parties who explicitly agreed to look only to the segregated assets of the venture. However, sometimes by statute, sometimes by judge-made rules within a statutory framework, corporation law undertook to settle many such matters, private agreements to the contrary notwithstanding. Thus in the middle and late nineteenth century statutes commonly limited the type of shares which corporations might create and definitively fixed the voting rights of shareholders, and some courts held that statutory provisions that corporations be managed by boards of directors precluded voting pools and other contracts by which stockholders might directly control management. Where corporation law thus settled what contract law might have allowed the parties to contrive by themselves, we do not confront elements of corporate status which derive uniquely from law in the sense that only law could create them. Rather, we confront special legal regulations of business behavior within the corporate frame. Such elements of corporate powers were not inherent in corporate status. They were in effect parts of a consideration exacted by law for creation of those elements which only the law could give.[11]

3. Law might provide a standard—but not a required—corporate package. It did so around the mid-nineteenth century when legislatures provided optional general incorporation acts but at the same time continued to grant special charters with different terms. At the turn of the century legislatures began to provide incorporation only under general acts; however, they began to stipulate elements which only law could create and to add other specifications, declaring that the latter should operate unless the parties stipulated otherwise in the corporate articles or bylaws. This kind of incorporation act combined features of franchise and regulation. In addition to creating for business as-

[11] Berle and Means, 131, 134, 136–37; Dodd (2), 977, and (7), 32, 36, 38, 40; Hornstein (4), 1:134; Rutledge, 308, 312, 337–40.

sociations such entity character as only law could give, such laws imposed qualified regulation of business behavior by preferring certain styles of organization unless the parties took a positive initiative otherwise.[12]

All three of these types of legislative action were involved in the development of public policy affecting the business corporation between 1780 and 1870. But at the time men did not see clearly that different values and different implications for community well-being were at stake in these various franchises. What particularly bred confusion and controversy was the contemporary failure to distinguish between the franchise to act as a corporate entity in law and franchises to engage in particular substantive lines of business or to enjoy particular privileges or immunities of substantive business action under law. The three types of legislative action did not run parallel but became interwoven, while the different types achieved prominence at different times. This interweaving reflected a mixture of desire, acceptance, and fear. We need to disentangle the positive and negative aspects of this record to understand the policy-making process and its products.

Given the normal inertias of the legislative process and the simplicity of the times, some strong, practical pressures were required to produce the growth in use of the corporation from the 1780's into the 1830's. The predominance of public-utility-type enterprises among this first generation of business corporations helps identify the positive factors at work. This society was early preoccupied with the challenge of economic growth. Its opportunities obviously outreached its current means. Highly individualistic in temper and focusing upon the market as an arena for individual striving, men were nonetheless aware that the desired economic development called for supporting institutions which only collective effort could provide.

Especially they felt the need to promote an increase in money and credit and in transportation facilities. So legislatures granted special privileges to set up note-issuing banks and to lay out canal, turnpike, and—from the 1830's—railroad rights of

[12] Berle and Means, 135–52; Dodd (2), 984; Hornstein (4), 1:188; Kuehnl, 140–42, 146–57; O'Neal, 1:127–28, note 18; Rutledge, 337–40.

way, together with the privilege of the eminent domain power and toll rights as aids in fostering such enterprises. Such grants delegated functions of public interest to private hands and reduced, if not completely obviated, direct intervention of the state. Direct state action was also important in the early nineteenth century; the success of the Erie Canal inspired much imitation in Pennsylvania and in the Ohio Valley. However, our concern is primarily with the growth of policy affecting the business corporation. Granted the direct interventions of the state in New York, Pennsylvania, and Ohio, the record also shows a large continuing reliance on delegation to private groups of provision of transport facilities and, even more so, of money and credit. This kind of delegation had great impetus behind it in the realities of the political as well as the economic situation. We felt the need to promote a volunteer muster of capital for sizable ventures at a time when fluid capital was scarce and there were severe practical limits on government's ability to tax in order to support direct intervention in the economy. There is circumstantial evidence of these pressures in the contemporary proliferation of special franchises for transportation and financial activity at the same time that government stood ready to promote development through subsidies in kind—through such substitutes for tax-derived cash as public lands subsidies and delegations of the power of eminent domain. Of similar implication were the grants of toll rights and of rights to make loans in the form of the lender's own bank notes; given the want of any strong official superintendence, such privileges were in practical effect delegations of power to levy private taxes on those dependent on the services; thus grants of such privileges promoted the raising of capital and at the same time avoided the direct compulsions of the state to such ends.[13]

The need was to encourage the volunteer muster not only of capital but also of promotional and managerial talent. By the early nineteenth century circumstances produced a rising demand and challenge for organizational skills. A growing popula-

[13] Broude, 9, 13; Bruchey, 128–29, 131; Cochran (2), 339, 345–47, 352, 355; Hurst (2), 59–70, and (4), 10, 38, 39, 171, 231, 274, 276–78; North, 101, 103; Scheiber, ch. 4.

tion, improving communications, and the creation of a working federalism fostered expanding markets and in turn brought the need for a better supply of money and credit; the career of Nicholas Biddle in the Second Bank of the United States bears witness to the need and the opportunities implicit in such facts. New machine technologies invited large-scale enterprises demanding greater skills in direction and technical operations than ever before; the growth first of the textile industry and then of trunk-line railroads brought the need of a new order of business direction. Quite apart from the fact that the social and political tradition favored reliance on broadly dispersed private, as compared with public, power, it was clear that the management vigor and skills demanded by the times would not come from government. An important inheritance from the American Revolution was a jealousy of official executive power, which made for a weak executive under state constitutions. Inexperience and want of tax resources also spelled weak, if not almost nonexistent, administrative capacity in government. However, if government could not directly supply a new quality of executive ability for economic growth, it did have the means to stimulate and arm the emergence of such leadership out of private energy and imagination by the inducements and opportunities offered through grants of corporate and special-action franchises.[14]

Franchises carrying special privileges of substantive business action—rights of way and toll rights or the authority to issue bank notes, for example—were the principal means by which legislatures delegated the muster of capital and entrepreneurial skills to private action. But many—and most of the important —special-action franchises were in fact granted to corporations. Evidently positive demand for the corporate instrument had some functional relation to the utilities found in special-action franchises. The corporation met the need to develop organization as a major economic asset by legitimating a combination of strong central direction and limited commitments. This combi-

[14] Cochran (1), ch. 6 and (2), 343, 350–51, 352, 355; Davis, 2:130; Goodrich, 284–87, 289; Govan, 84–88, 92–97; Freeman Hunt, 1:570; Hurst (1), 382–84.

nation constituted the business reality within the legal idea of the corporation as a separate working entity.

By the 1850's, even in its simpler, more restricted forms, corporate structure implied a high value put upon organizational vitality. Corporation law early favored business arrangements which centralized decision making, gave it considerable assurance of tenure, and armed it for vigorous maneuver. Shareholder decisions, it was soon established, should normally be by simple majority. Active management should be concentrated in a board of directors; stockholders did not have owners' rights over the particular assets of a going corporate enterprise; unless exhibiting gross abuse of power or breach of faith, directors' decisions governed the regular course of the business. Continuity was important to effective organization. Insofar as law could contribute to an undisturbed flow of operations, it favored strong central direction of pooled assets; capacity for indefinite life, uninterrupted by change of shareholders, was an enterprise-continuity value peculiar to the corporate form. A board of directors must do its business as a body, not as individuals. But—in significant departure from common law injunctions that agents might not delegate their roles—for ready dispatch of business a corporate board might designate officers and agents for the firm's business and might even turn over interim decision making in the regular course of dealings to an executive committee of its membership. We must not exaggerate the extent to which corporation law centralized decision making at first. Considerable distrust and controversy attended the special-franchise, special-charter era. This atmosphere generated limitations. For example, flexible continuity was hindered by a common law rule that a unanimous vote of stockholders was necessary to amend corporate articles, and—perhaps because charters often set sharp limits on corporate life—early legislation made no other provision for amendment. Moreover, courts were at first hesitant to recognize implied powers in boards of directors, and only in the second half of the nineteenth century were they ready to find that management enjoyed such implied authority as might be necessary or proper to their business ends.

But such restrictive features proved not to be in the main line of policy. On balance, and from the outset, the corporation was an instrument to provide firm central direction for the enterprising use of pooled assets.[15]

The matching element which made the corporate form so useful an instrument was its facilities for limited commitments by those who would contribute capital to the undertaking, whether by fresh investment or, in greater degree, by plowing back earnings into operations in which they were already involved. By legitimating a distinct operating fund, legally recognized as a contracting, title-holding entity with capacity to sue and be sued, the law helped promoters multiply particularized opportunities for investment. In an economy lacking sophisticated capital markets, such as commercial banks, investment bankers, and other institutionalized financial intermediaries and stock markets would later provide, this was no mean gain. Besides helping furnish targets of opportunity, the corporate form encouraged the muster or retention of resources by offering investors an assured frame of limited commitments of various sorts. The corporate share structure helped define the limits of mutual commitment among shareholders. The obverse of creating a firm, substantially autonomous center of direction for corporate business was assurance to investors that they had a vehicle for limiting their investments of time and energy as well as of money.[16]

Tradition assigns as a prime limited-commitment inducement to use of the corporation the limited liability of shareholders to outsiders for debts of the enterprise. The tradition has substance and has gained more substance with time. But the record requires qualification.

[15] Angell and Ames, 121–38; 251–56; 266–69; Baker and Cary, 353; Dodd (23), 112, 190, 519–21; Hornstein (4), 1:225, 227; O'Neal, 1:205–8; Stevens (1), 68, and 68, note 41, 69, 72, 567, 647–51, 655, 656–57.

[16] Cadman, 39, 40, 41; Davis, 1:447, and 2:121, 158, 160, 241; Hartz (1), 75; Heath, 322; Kuehnl, 61; New York, 518 (remarks of Mr. Stow); Primm, 54, 56, 57. On the relatively greater importance of retained earnings and bank loans than of equity capital, *cf.* Bruchey, 143–47, 151–53; Cochran (2), 345–47, 350, 352, 354.

Though the matter was in some doubt in the late eighteenth century, judge-made law, as it developed between about 1810 and 1860, made clear that a corporation charter conferred limited liability by implication in the absence of clear provision to the contrary. As the use of the business corporation widened in the span from about 1850 to 1880, statutes supported the earlier presumption of limited liability by the courts. With the notable exception of banks, legislation now granted shareholders unqualified immunity against claims of third persons upon the enterprise. Legislatures offset this clarified status of shareholders by imposing regulations of corporate financial policy—limiting sources of dividends and retirement of shares, for example—to protect the integrity of the corporate fund for creditors. But this closer attention to the security of the corporation's own working fund only accented the insulation of the investors from outside claimants.[17]

Because these parts of the record fit so readily the twentieth-century stereotype of the shareholder's protected position, it is easy to overlook significant qualifications which marked statutory policy in the first half of the nineteenth century. The same years (1810–60) which saw the courts establish a firm presumption that limited liability was granted by statutory silence also witnessed imposition of considerable explicit statutory liability on corporate shareholders. Leading industrial states put qualified liability on shareholders to third-party claimants against the corporation—sometimes to the amount of the shareholders' unpaid stock subscriptions, sometimes to double the shareholder's investment, sometimes in proportion to the investor's holdings with or without a stated maximum liability, sometimes for particular debts (as, notably, for debts owed for labor). True, the legislative pattern as a whole implied a steady desire to make incorporation available on terms which would foster investment by limiting commitments; legislatures rarely

---

[17] Before the 1850's: Angell and Ames, 38, 597, 613; Dodd (23), 85, 227, 369–71, 373, 374; Hartz (1), 256, 257; Stevens (1), 840, 841; *cf.* Handlin, 147; Livermore, 281, note 27. From the 1850's: Berle and Means 127, 130–31; Dodd (8), 254, 268, 274; Katz, 181–83; Latty (2), 375.

imposed absolute liability on stockholders for debts of the firm, and when they created qualified liability, they usually did so only as to particular types of enterprise (as the special liability of bank shareholders for redemption of the bank's note issues). Nonetheless, legislatures subjected corporate shareholders to enough liability through the span from about 1810–1860 that we must doubt the inducement of limited liability as the prime explanation for the growing popularity of the corporate form of business.[18] Moreover, in corporations of relatively few shareholders and relatively modest assets—whose number tended to grow in the late nineteenth century—a familiar fact of business practice enters to generate further skepticism about the extent to which stockholder limited liability promoted incorporation. For the small close-held corporation, a third-party creditor—and especially one lending working capital—would typically require the personal endorsements of shareholders on the firm's notes.[19] Thus as a matter of both law and business practice, there seems to be good reason to think that the other limited-commitment opportunities facilitated by corporate organization (defined purposes, defined shares, assurance of limited drafts upon investor time and energy) played as substantial a role in the growing popularity of incorporation as did formal legal limits on shareholder responsibility for debts.

The heart of the matter is that the corporation was an attractive instrument for business because it provided this combination of firm direction and limited commitment. However, examination of several hundred special charters of the mid-nineteenth-century decades reveals another practical impulse back of the growing resort to incorporation. The bustle of the times —the bursting expansion of enterprise in number, variety, risks, and problems of technical and marketing change—put a premium on improvisation and quick response to opportunity. The law of corporate organization in this country kept developing

[18] Angell and Ames, 37–38, 602, 613; Cadman, 103, 126, 127; Dodd (23), 230, 231, 241, 343, 344, 356–66, 374–77, 381, 391, 393, 398, 437; Hartz (1), 257; Heath, 316–18; Hornstein (4), 1:20, 39; Primm, 57, 58, 61; Stevens (1), 838–41.

[19] Dewing, 1:36; Hornstein (4), 1:49; Hurst (4), 862, note 104; Reynolds, 134; *cf.* Dodd (22), 390.

over a span of nearly two hundred years, and the process was obviously not over in the 1960's. The business corporation was far from a fully formed instrument in the 1860's. But development moved fast, especially from the 1830's into the 1850's. From the outset the corporate charter had at least a sharply defined form in law, emphasized by the consistent practice of putting charters in the statutory mould. Thus, in years when their normal pragmatism was heightened by the press of events, businessmen valued incorporation because it made available a standardized, legitimated form of organization, which they could take pretty much as a package. Implicit testimony to this impulse behind the spread of incorporation was the early enactment of stripped-down charters, which did hardly more than declare named incorporators to be a corporate body, leaving it to contemporary judge-made or general statute law to fill in most of the incidents of the status.[20] Typical—and at first appearance contrary to the idea of standardization—was the growth in the amount of detail put into special charters by mid-century. The combined evidence of hundreds upon hundreds of special charters with the elaboration of provisions on organization and powers written into these charters might be read as showing that the moving impulse was to tailor each charter to the particular desires of particular promoters. But closer reading shows relatively little variety spawned by all this print. The bulk of the content of most special charters tends to fall quickly into stock patterns.[21] The practical impulse behind the continued increase in number and detail of special charters seems to have been mainly the wish to avoid certain features of the optional general incorporation acts, which were becoming more common by mid-century—tight limits on capitalization, for example, and requirements that certain facts about the firm's operations be made a matter of public record. But whatever it was that they did not like about the available general incorporation acts, promoters and their lawyers did not strive for much variety in the internal organization of the companies.[22] The subsurface standardization of "special" charters reinforces the conclusion that

20 Hurst (4), 195; Kuehnl, 153.
21 Dodd (23), 198; Hurst (4), 195, 274, 417.
22 Hurst (4), 417–22; Kuehnl, 146–49, 155–57.

the corporation was valued substantially for its utility as a certain kind of generally well-defined organization.

In bold contrast to the steady practice of granting a special charter of incorporation to most businessmen who sought one was recurrent political controversy over the social acceptability of such corporate status. Controversy flared episodically, from the battle over repeal of the charter of the Bank of North America in Pennsylvania in 1785–86 to the contest over rechartering the Second Bank of the United States in the mid-1830's, and beyond. Especially between 1830 and 1860 anti-charter feeling was a staple support of Jacksonian politics.[23] This confused combat offers instructive lessons in the waste which the development of public policy may involve when legal processes produce unreal issues, wrong issues, or deflected attention. William Gouge, in his *Short History of Paper Money and Banking in the United States* (1833) offers a summary which embodies the prime sources of confusion:

Against corporations of every kind, the objection may be brought that whatever power is given to them is so much taken from either the government or the people. As the object of charters is to give to members of companies powers which they would not possess in their individual capacity, the very existence of monied corporations is incompatible with equality of rights. . . . Such are the inherent defects of corporations that they can never succeed, except when the laws or circumstances give them a monopoly or advantages partaking of the nature of a monopoly. Sometimes they are protected by direct inhibitions to individuals to engage in the same business. Sometimes they are protected by an exemption from liabilities to which individuals are subjected. Sometimes the extent of their capital or their credit gives them control of the market. They cannot, even then, work as cheap as the individual trader, but they can afford to throw away enough money in the contest to ruin the individual trader, and then they have the market to themselves.[24]

Muddled together here are objections based on (1) egalitarian values, (2) balance-of-power values, and (3) values of func-

[23] Govan, chs. 13–20; Hammond, 54–63; Hofstadter, 56–57, 63–66; Meyers, 199–203.

[24] Gouge, 17. On Gouge: Hammond, 298, 343–44; Schumpeter, 711, note 15.

tional efficiency. Gouge embodies the heart of the confusion of mid-nineteenth-century debate when he links a particular attack on banks to an indiscriminate attack on the corporate instrument in any use or with any character. It took another generation to disentangle the questions of special-action franchises from those of corporate status proper, which Gouge brought under a single attack.

In a mobile society of relatively simple economic and social circumstances equality under the law was a standard of great emotional as well as rational appeal. Thus it was not surprising that egalitarian claims were raised early against the business corporation. However, egalitarian distrust of the corporation derived from two different concerns, which eventually produced different responses.

One type of attack in the name of equality was upon the grant of corporate entity itself. The insistence that only a positive act of the sovereign might confer corporate status stood in stark contrast to the broad sweep which the general law of contract offered for private business arrangements.[25] Gouge strikes at these uniquely law-given incidents when he finds corporations inconsistent with equality of rights because "the object of charters is to give to members of companies powers which they would not possess in their individual capacity." Thus broadly phrased, the attack seems to challenge the social acceptability of corporate status under any circumstance in a society where the individual's well-being is the ultimate criterion of legitimate power. But the capacity of a business association to act effectively in law as an entity—to make contracts, for example, and to receive, hold, and transfer title to land—carried no value implications other than those of a useful, matter-of-fact procedure to aid transactions.[26] Somewhat different was the immunity which corporation law might give stockholders against personal liability for the firm's debts; Gouge may have this incident as one of his targets when he is critical because sometimes corpo-

[25] *Cf.* Hurst (2), 12, 15.
[26] Dodd (23), 48, 50; Henderson, 37, 38, 45. The capacity of corporations to qualify as litigants in federal courts raised questions of federalism rather than of incorporation. *Cf.* Dodd (23), 50.

rations (that is, men-organized-into-corporations) "are protected by an exemption from liabilities to which individuals are subjected." Here, presumably justified by the social interest in promoting economic venture, law made its own allocation of gains and risks of enterprise and thus affected substantive interests beyond a point of mere convenience. Like Gouge's, some other early attacks on corporations in the name of equality appear to have arisen simply because—in its entity character and in the limited liability of shareholders—a corporate enterprise could operate by procedures and with legal incidents different from those familiar in individual trading.[27] But unless we dogmatically identified equality with exclusively individual action, no egalitarian principle required that we outlaw a useful instrument of associated action. Of course, we did not dogmatically foreswear associated business activity; the law of partnership, agency, and trusts, as well as the swelling volume of special charters, amply testified to the contrary.[28] The compatibility of corporate status with individual equality under law raised issues of procedure rather than of substance. There were no reasons of structure or function why law might not confer entity status on an indefinitely large number of business associations and limited liability on stockholders as investors in an indefinitely large number of pooled ventures. The valid egalitarian point was simply that, if corporate entity was a useful instrument of regular business, and if stockholders' limited liability was a useful means of encouraging venture, these devices should be available by a simple procedure on equal terms to all who saw use for them in ordinary business associations. That this answer made principled as well as practical sense was shown by the fact that the individualistic egalitarian objection passed out of the main current of Jacksonian polemics against corporations.[29] A different fear was that advantages of incorporation might foster such asset concentrations as to upset a desirable dispersion of power in the marketplace. But this concern was for the general social structure rather than for individual equality.

[27] Davis, 2:203; Hammond, 54–56; Hartz (1), 70; Henderson, 38, 42.
[28] Dodd (2), 981–85, and (8), 258, 259; Hornstein (3), 436.
[29] Hofstadter, 63; Meyers, 200, 203.

The general incorporation laws—first, as optional alternatives to special charters and, then, by the seventies and eighties as the exclusive channels to corporate status—put to rest the individualistic-egalitarian issue. But the movement to this outcome was not without costs while we fumbled for a realistic definition of the issue. Appeals to an abstract, absolutist individualism confused ends and means. The confusion obscured the fact that for many, if not most, business purposes corporate status as such raised no issues other than those of instrumental efficiency. Also, this delay in seeing the issue as one of general utility rather than of special privilege delayed perception that corporate organization could be simply an extension of freedom of contract. All features of corporate organization were not necessarily the product of the law's franchise; many matters, as those of share structure and the internal division of powers, were such as men might otherwise contrive to their own designs in unincorporated association under the general law of contract. Insofar as corporation law intervened on such points, its intervention amounted to a form of social regulation of business behavior rather than to creation of incidents uniquely in the gift of the sovereign.[30]

A second kind of attack on the corporation in the name of equality was not really directed at corporate status but at franchises allowing the grantees to carry on a particular business or to enjoy particular privileges or immunities which law denied the general run of individuals or groups. In large measure such special-action franchises were given only to business corporations; this might be a matter of practice, as it was with railroads, or of declared policy, as it came to be with note-issuing banks. In any event, where such situations came into controversy on appeals to standards of equality, the heart of the challenge was most often to the grant of some special-action franchise and not to the grant of corporate existence. There was functional sense behind this shape of the issue. Egalitarian attacks on incorporation for ordinary business purposes quickly faded before the realization that in that context the corporation

---

[30] Berle (10), 935–36; Chayes, 35; Davis, 1:428, 430, 439; Henderson, 68–69.

presented questions of convenience and utility rather than of justice. Conversely, no major egalitarian attack was leveled at railroads or note-issuing banks merely because they did business in corporate form: in these cases operational imperatives clearly presented questions not only of convenience and utility but also of need; the corporate form was a clearly superior, if not almost indispensable, instrument for mustering and disciplining large amounts of capital and allowing dependable continuity for its use.[31] Concern for the impact on the general balance of power sometimes raised issues of corporate organization where corporations held great power by virtue of their other special franchises. Thus the opposition to rechartering the Second Bank of the United States included the professed objections that foreigners might be shareholders and that power within the organization did not fairly represent sectional interests in the national economy.[32] But, again, concern with the social balance of power raised issues quite different from those appealing to the standard of equality under law.

Gouge is criticizing grants of special-action franchises rather than grants of corporate status when—echoing Adam Smith—he claims that corporations are so inherently inefficient "that they can never succeed, except when the laws or circumstances give them a monopoly or advantages partaking of the nature of a monopoly." [33] Once more, the criticism mingles fear for the balance of power with distaste for law-given special privilege. But Gouge makes a special target of the law's favors: "Sometimes [corporations] . . . are protected by direct inhibitions to individuals to engage in the same business." And his criticism extends beyond the grant of limited liability to stockholders, as he adds that "sometimes they are protected by an exemption from liabilities to which individuals are subjected."

Compared with other values recognized in contemporary practice, egalitarian attacks on "monopoly" and other special-

---

[31] Cadman, 63, 64, 66; Cochran and Miller, 67–76; Davis, 2:102–3; Gregg, 130, 131, 137; Hammond, 28, 572, 594; Henderson, 45, 46; Kuehnl, 122; Kuznets, 55; Livermore, 248.

[32] Govan, 201, 202; Hammond 407, 408. But *cf*. Wilburn, ch. 8.

[33] *Cf*. Adam Smith, 2:229 (bk. V, ch. 1).

action franchises blurred the pattern of public policy. Exclusive privileges might be functional with respect to desired social ends. Explicit monopolies, or protections against competition, were rare. Most often grantees obtained a practical monopoly in greater or less degree because legislators would not multiply a given kind of grant or because the profitable opportunities in a given area of trade or service were practically so limited that the first-chartered groups preempted the field. Some degree of monopoly might serve the public interest; too many dams would impair navigation and power uses of a stream; an indefinite number of note-issuing banks endangered a reliable money supply; if franchises were to attract private capital and directing talent to public-utility-type enterprises, in place of direct state action, they must be sufficiently limited to promise profit. To the extent that limited availability was necessary to attract private venture to serve public need, the egalitarian objection could not be met by creating general access to such privileges. Mid-nineteenth-century readiness to use franchises to delegate the service of public interest meant that we could not escape creating unequal positions by law. The situation was inherently ambiguous because narrowly focused private interest aggressively sought such franchises to profit by them. Egalitarian slogans did not solve the resulting problems, which were issues of structuring social power rather than of achieving equality among individuals. The relevant call was not for equal access to opportunities inherently limited, but for responsible procedures to assess how public interest might be served by granting some persons special positions. Or, in another view, substantial, not merely formal, equality required "special" treatment of some situations because the situations could not be indefinitely multiplied, as the grant of corporate status could be. A simplistic yes or no would not meet the issue. Talk of objectionable inequalities introduced by corporations of every kind deflected attention from the true problem. It was all the easier to deflect attention because the institutional machinery was poorly adapted to grappling with the real issues. To determine on what terms and on what kind of record public interest would be served by grants of special privilege would have taxed more experienced legislatures and would have required the help of more sophisticated executive and administrative apparatus than the nineteenth-century states possessed. Jackson's veto of the new charter for the Second Bank of the United States dramatized the incapacity to handle these matters effectively, for he undertook by a simple negative to shelve issues which called for positive action under continuing public supervision. Not the least costly aspect of the mid-century confusion between grants of corporate status and grants of special-action privilege was that it postponed coming to grips with the creation of adequate legislative standards and adequate administrative means to deal with problems which the play of the market could not adequately handle.[34]

Interwoven with claims that incorporation violated a canon of equality among individuals were sharply felt fears about, and interest in, the private economic power which the corporation could help muster. Fear for the balance of power spurred controversy more frequent, livelier, and more persistent than that centered on arguments over individual equality. Thus Gouge takes as the premise for his broad attack the proposition that "against corporations of every kind, the objection may be brought that whatever power is given to them is so much taken from either the government or the people." This concern—that power is taken from "either the government or the people"— goes to the general structure of society rather than to the relative position of individuals. True, the themes are related in origin and appeal. In the eighteenth and early nineteenth centuries in most people's experience the society was one of considerable equality in fact or in promise; this view fostered a public opinion instinctively jealous of concentrated power of any sort.[35] Political tradition reinforced this bias; we believed in dispersion of official power among different agencies, with representative assemblies as prime policy makers, subject to formal constitu-

[34] Berle and Means, 128; Bruchey, 129–31; Cadman, 226; Cochran and Miller, 77–81; Davis, 2:320; Dodd (23), 205, 206, 241–46, 403; Goodrich, 286, 287; Hammond, 67; Hurst (4) 214–25, 228, 231, 233, 236–39; Kirkland, 1:267–73.

[35] McConnell, 5–8; Meyers, 15–17, 21, 40, 78–89; Henry Nash Smith, 133, 135, 140–42; Williams, 409–11.

tional limitations.[36] Egalitarian faith provided powerful motives for attending to the balance of power. On the other hand, talk of balance of power invited attention to large institutional arrangements and to broad shifts in social relations, reaching into more complex problems of values and procedures than were comprehended by simplistic condemnation of corporations because they were not individual traders. Thus, over the long span there was more matter for political combat in concern for the social balance of power than in appeals only to the criterion of individual equality. And, in fact, arguments over corporations' impact on the balance of power persisted in varying forms into the twentieth century, while individualist-egalitarian protests died away when general incorporation acts became the norm after the 1870's.

However, development of balance-of-power issues shared with the course of egalitarian complaints contemporary confusion between grants of the corporate franchise and grants of special-action franchises. Special-action franchises generated balance-of-power concerns in proportion as they put the grantees in positions in which many other persons and activities were dependent in critical degree on how the grantees used their special privileges and immunities. This practical power over other people derived not from being a corporation but from having rights (often, in practice if not by formal declaration, rights carrying a significant extent of monopoly) to lay out a railroad right of way and fix charges for carriage, or to issue bank notes intended as a general medium of exchange, or to improve and control navigation on a key waterway. It would help considerably in exercising such special-action franchises if the grantees might organize their business in corporate form. But almost always the substantial battles of the special-charter era were not over incidents of corporate existence but over law-given privileges to engage in particular kinds of business activity which the general run of men were not legally free to undertake, and on which other men found themselves crucially dependent. Thus almost all public controversy over special franchises concerned banks, railroads, and insurance companies or on a

[36] *The Federalist,* nos. 10 (Madison) and 51 (Hamilton).

smaller scale toll bridges, turnpikes, power dams, and navigation improvements; the heart of controversy was not corporate-
ness but banking, railroading, insuring, or some other business
operation on which an environing community found itself peculiarly dependent. Before the late nineteenth century the contests
which enlisted substantial opposing forces and achieved noto-
riety were not over corporations in retail or wholesale trade or
in manufacturing or natural-resource extraction. Thus contests
did not arise over corporate business centered on economic activity which the ordinary law of the marketplace—contract and
property law—left open to anyone. Contests centered on economic activity which the law did not hold open to all comers,
where the state's license was required for lawful pursuit of the
activity itself.[37]

These were the facts. But contemporaries often did not so see
them, and—as with the purely egalitarian issue—they tended to
blur the issues by confounding grants of corporate status with licenses for particular substantive economic activity. We can
measure the extent of the confusion by noting that so acute a
lawyer as Mr. Chief Justice Taney could fall into it. Speaking
for a Court majority in 1837 in the *Charles River Bridge* case,
Taney ruled that a franchise conferring privileges not open to
the public should be strictly construed against the grantees in
favor of preserving public rights; the Court refused to find that
a statutory grant of a toll-bridge franchise carried implied mo-
nopolistic protection against erection of another bridge nearby.
The decision put competing values in sensible order, as was attested by the ready adoption of the principle the country over.
Yet Taney's opinion confused the definition of what was at
stake. The Court should deny an implied monopoly grant, said
Taney, in order to preserve "the power of the several States, in
relation to the corporations they have chartered," for the issues
were "pregnant with important consequences, not only to the individuals who are concerned in the corporate franchises, but to
the communities in which they exist."[38] However, the real

[37] Dodd (23), 365, 366, 376, 388; Hurst (4), 410–11.
[38] Proprietors of the Charles River Bridge v. Proprietors of the Warren
Bridge, 11 Peters 420, 536 (U.S. 1837). *Cf.* Handlin, 213, 237.

stake in the *Charles River Bridge* case was not the bridge proprietors' franchise to be a corporation, but their franchise to build and operate a bridge and charge tolls for its use. Similar confusion appears in Gouge. He makes a broad attack on corporations as such. Yet, significantly, his specific targets are banks; the core objections to banks were not that they were corporations, but that they had capacity to create paper money and to control credit.[39]

Here, again, practice came closer to reality than did debate. While talk confused the questions posed by incorporation and special-action franchises, legislatures wrote into turnpike, railroad, navigation-improvement, insurance, and banking charters regulatory provisions unlike any put into the general run of charters for industrial and trading corporations. Distinctive to transportation company charters were statutory stipulations for provision of promised facilities (that, on pain of forfeiture, minimum capital be subscribed and paid in, operations begin within some specified time, and works be kept in good order and not abandoned), for tolls to be within set minimum and maximum levels, to be fair and reasonable, and to be conditioned on substantial service, and for certain operations reports to be regularly filed. Distinctive to bank charters were particular requirements as to minimum capital paid in, specie reserves, personal liability of bank directors for various kinds of misconduct, special liability of stockholders for debts of the bank, and the rendering of reports and the opening of books to legislative inquiry. Distinctive to insurance company charters was a slow elaboration of special financial regulations, directed at creating an adequate insurance fund and protecting its integrity against careless or fraudulent diversion.[40] Through the nineteenth century such special regulatory provisions were at best of limited effect. They dealt with problems technically complex, difficult and varied in detail, and so woven into the shifting context of a rapidly grow-

[39] *Cf.* Hammond, 328, 341, 343–44, 353, 359; Hartz (1), 67, 68, 254, 255, 257; Livermore, 246–47, 251, 252.

[40] Cadman, 369–72, 374, 390; Dodd (23), 158–62, 203, 205, 208, 209, 212, 241–46, 344–46; Hurst (4), 214–20, 275–77; Kimball, 68, 130; Kuehnl, 56; Primm, 40–47, 52.

ing economy as to require continuing, specialized, expert supervision. Thus, the regulatory goals set by legislatures could be achieved only through steady, strong, capable executive or administrative effort. In the nineteenth-century situation it was almost inevitable that we would not provide the necessary executive or administrative apparatus. From the American Revolution we inherited a stubborn distrust of committing power to the executive. In an economy hardpressed for fluid capital, taxes were difficult to raise for any public ventures let alone for the support of a swelling bureaucracy. Expanding markets and evolving technology multiplied demand for managerial skills beyond what the market could supply for private undertakings, apart from government's needs.[41] Nonetheless, the special regulatory provisions included in transport, banking, and insurance charters represented significant growth in public policy, even though the want of administrative machinery deprived them of much immediate operational effect. Recognition that particular lines of business called for specialized responses in public policy was an indispensable first step toward combining a perceptive definition of, with adequate means for realizing, the public interest. Implicit in the regulatory terms peculiar to certain kinds of corporate charters was the rudimentary beginning of a law of public utilities.[42] We should not be condescending toward the nineteenth century's groping movement; as late as the 1960's public policy toward key industries was still characterized by blurred definition of goals (for example, debates over peacetime uses of atomic energy or the values which should govern communication by radio and television) and grossly inadequate administration (for example, the great disparities among states in quality of regulation of electric power, telephone rates, and the insurance business). The mid-nineteenth-century policy record might have been better, however, had contemporary critics not confused analysis by identifying corporate status rather than special industrial or commercial position as the source of bal-

[41] Cadman, 374; Dodd (23) 201, 203, 212, 276, 279; Hartz (1), 33, 151–53, 155–59, 170, 191, 204–6, 262–63, 266, 292–95, 310; Hibbard, 560; Hurst (4), 227, 229, 231, 239.

[42] Frankfurter, 82–85; Glaeser, 33–34.

ance-of-power problems. This approach slowed the growth of realistic policy by misdirecting attention. To emphasize corporate
status made the issue seem one of simplistic legislative decision
—to grant or not to grant a certain organizational form by statute. This view encouraged lawmakers to evade the harder problems of more specifically defining public interest and providing
adequate administrative implementation.

In one respect nineteenth-century concern over imbalance of
power did refer to feared effects of corporate organization of
business as such, and not to the impact of special-action franchises. This anxiety was for the relation of corporate organization to size of firms and the bearing of size on the market as an
institution of social control.

In effect our tradition relied as much on the impersonally
competitive market to prevent abuse of private economic power
as on constitutional limitations to prevent abuse of public
power. Indeed, the idea of constitutionally limited government
—with its insistence that the state should use its power only for
purposes of public interest and should not intervene in affairs
merely of private concern—assumed that most business was
"private" precisely because the nonofficial discipline of the market existed to keep oppressive or wasteful practices from reaching such proportions as to make them properly subjects of
"public" attention. This proposition was present, though mostly
implied, in the earlier years when the simple conditions of society offered little occasion to bring the matter to explicit statement. Locke grounded the moral legitimacy of private property
on the assumption that men apply their labor to resources in situations "where there is enough and as good left in common for
others." Jefferson urged that the guiding principle of legal order
should be to achieve "a wise and frugal government, which shall
restrain men from injuring one another, which shall leave them
otherwise free to regulate their own pursuits of industry and improvement, and shall not take from the mouth of labor the
bread it has earned." We reconciled our principles with the federal government's monopoly of the country's principal fixed asset—government ownership of almost all western land—by rapidly putting the lands up for public auction or otherwise dispos-

ing of them on terms calculated to bring as much acreage as possible into private fee simple ownership as fast as possible; in other words, to put the land on the market. Of like import was a leading argument in the New York constitutional convention of 1846 for abolishing remnants of feudal tenure, that "there should be no more restrictions placed upon the alienation of real estate than upon personal estate. Property was improved by passing from hand to hand." [43]

Such views implied dispersion of private economic decision making among actors so numerous, so matched in means, and so equal under law that only the impersonal, cumulative impact of their total strivings would determine the allocation of resources and distribution of rewards that would emerge from their efforts. Well past the mid-nineteenth century we were so short of money, men, and managerial talent relative to our opportunities that our main reliance on the market was to promote efficient use of resources. Not until the emergence of great financial and industrial combinations from the 1880's on did events press us to emphasize the market as a control upon private power in finance, trade, and manufacture generally. Yet, the market's function of maintaining a balance of power was implicit in the market's function of promoting efficient allocation of resources; over-all efficiency would be improved because the participants lacked practical ability to manipulate transactions to promote their narrower interests.[44] By the mid-nineteenth century the balance-of-power function of the general market had explicit recognition in decisions asserting the power of courts to review private covenants not to compete, incident to the sale of a business or the end of an employment, and to hold invalid agreements found to be unreasonable restraints of trade.[45] However, the most substantial witness to the weight early put on the market as a balance-of-power factor was the recurrent controversy over special-action franchises—right-of-way

[43] Locke, ch. 5; Jefferson, in Richardson, 1:324; New York, 523. *Cf.* Hibbard, 4, 5, 547, 549, 555; Peterson, 19, 22, 76, 80, 255; Sabine, 527–28; Schlatter, 156–57.

[44] Knight, 258–59.

[45] Freund, 73; Thorelli, 38–50.

monopolies, toll grants, limited charters for bank privileges. It was their elements of antimarket monopoly power as much as their departure from the canon of equal rights which made such franchises attractive targets for pamphleteers and stump speakers. We delegated functions of broad public interest to private franchise holders in order to get jobs done. At the same time—recognizing the potential power conferred—we were distrustful of our delegates precisely because their special privileges of action put them outside usual market disciplines and hence gave them some of the character of sovereignty.[46]

Thus, through the middle nineteenth century one line of attack on use of the corporate device for business organization was the charge that it would tend to subvert market control of private economic power. In one form this attack expressed fear that corporate organization would dilute the sense of personal moral and legal responsibility among those directing business enterprises and so encourage them in antisocial action. This was the most specific and objective meaning of warnings that corporations were "soulless." The charge could as well be leveled against individuals operating in the market under the whip of impersonal competition, calculated to blind them to all but the search for maximized short-run profit. The comparison eluded contemporary critics who feared the corporation's want of soul.[47]

Most often the fear expressed was that the corporate form would facilitate such concentrations of assets as to allow corporations to overpower the individuals or smaller unincorporated groups with whom they dealt. Gouge warns that "sometimes the extent of [corporations'] capital or of their credit gives them control of the market. They cannot, even then, work as cheap as the individual trader, but they can afford to throw away enough money in the contest to ruin the individual trader, and

[46] Hartz (1), 71–72, 314–19; Henderson, 21, 34, 35; Stevens (1), 5; *cf*. Chayes, 36–37.

[47] Cadman, 78 and 78, note 192; Chandler (1), 272; Dodd (23), 4–6; Hammond, 54–56, 608; Handlin, 214; Hartz (1), 61; Kuehnl, 220; *cf*. Cochran (1), 92, 93; Timberg, 550. For a contrary position: Hartz (1), 74; Knight, 270.

then they have the market to themselves." The same concern found expression in arguments that law must offset the "artificial" power with which incorporated firms could overpower workers and small businessmen. An early individualist-egalitarian dogma criticized corporations simply because they had legal capacities not held by individual traders; this objection faded out about mid-century, to be succeeded by the worry that by their special capacities for business maneuvering corporations would drive small men from the field. In this later form, the objection was to the corporations' impact on the competitive market rather than to values of individualism as such.[48]

As Gouge's comments indicate, it was precisely the key organizational utilities of the corporate form which it was feared would allow corporate business to upset a desirable market balance of power. In corporate form men could muster capital in greater concentrations than they could by other means ("the extent of . . . capital or of their credit gives them control of the market") and could exercise strong, perhaps ruthless, central command over it ("they can afford to throw away enough money in the contest to ruin the individual trader"). The mid-nineteenth-century indictments customarily used these emotionally charged generalities, furnishing little detail of just how the general incidents of corporate status would be used to unseat market controls of private power. But there is implied confirmation and some further definition of contemporary fears in various restrictive, or regulatory, provisions first written into special corporate charters and then into the optional general incorporation acts of mid-century and finally made parts of standard general acts which provided the exclusive modes of incorporation in the 1870's and 1880's. Thus legislation early required that corporate articles define a limiting purpose or field of operations for the corporate enterprise. Limitation of purpose commonly applied to corporations for trade and industry, as well as to those embarking on business of a public utility character. But

---

[48] Cadman, 70, 80, note 202; Davis, 2:304, 205; Dodd (23), 394, 395, note 8, 403, 414–15, 416, 432; Hammond, 54, 608; Hartz (1), 60, 69, 72; Heath, 323; Paul, 52, 53, 54–59; Stocking and Watkins, 18, note 8.

fear that corporate business might reach a socially dangerous breadth of ambition surfaced particularly in charters for banks and insurance corporations, in expressed prohibitions against their engaging in other lines of trade. Functionally related to limitations of corporate purpose were the denial by courts that one corporation might own the stock of another without explicit statutory authority, and the granting by legislatures of such permission only rarely and in limited situations until New Jersey's innovating laws of the 1880's and 1890's. Special and general statutes commonly set dollar ceilings on the corporations' capitalization or on the value of the assets they might hold. Of course, such limitations might be relaxed by later amendment, but the necessity of going back to the legislature for such action was in itself a potential regulation of corporate power. Another expression of concern for the unsettling effect corporate enterprise might have on the social balance of power was the prevalence of limits set on the years for which a corporation might exist. Such limits did not destroy the utility of continuity within the appointed span, uninterrupted by voluntary or involuntary changes in shareholders. But they were another device to subject corporations to recurrent legislative scrutiny.[49]

These restrictive elements built into corporate status—on sanctioned business purposes, on capitalization and assets, on length of corporate life—commonly applied to corporations organized for general trade and industrial enterprises as well as to those formed for public-utility-type business, such as transportation, finance, and water supply. Thus these limitations imply a concern for balance of power arising out of the potentials of the corporate device itself, and not simply out of possession of special privileges of substantive economic action, such as toll rights or capacity to issue bank notes. The breadth of their adoption indicates concession to some substantial opinion distrustful of the corporation as such. But there are three reasons for assigning limited operating importance to the restrictions.

[49] Berle and Means, 131, 134, 136; Brandeis (1), 549–56; Cadman, 232, 233, 241, 242, 244; Davis, 1:380, 429, 430, 439, 442; Dodd (7), 31, 32, 36, 38, 40, (8), 274, 275, and (10), 6, 7; Hornstein (4), 1:26, 125, 134; Rutledge, 306–8.

1. Inclusion of such limitations was accompanied by legislative generosity in making corporate status available to almost any petitioners who sought it for any purpose not plainly unlawful. The exceptions almost all concerned banking and transport, where the pressures to limit chartering typically came from jealousy of monopoly rather than from distrust of corporate status. Legislative records continued to show only rare instances in which charters were refused in the special-charter decades, and both the optional and the exclusive general incorporation acts permitted men to incorporate on generous terms for almost any lawful business purpose. In this perspective, the restrictive provisions appear as never more than marginal limitations on a dominant policy of accepting incorporation as a socially useful instrument of economic growth.[50]

2. Though these limitations were applied to corporations for general trade and industry, until the end of the nineteenth century there was no substantial controversy concerning business associations which did not involve public-utility-type corporations with special-action franchises. The active fear of strong central management, concentrated resources, and indefinite enterprise life was attached in the nineteenth century peculiarly to firms which coupled the corporate franchise with franchises for substantive action not legally open to businessmen in general.[51]

3. On the typically scant record of the background of state legislative policy, there is a good deal of ambiguity about the public policy objectives of these restrictive provisions. There is some basis for interpreting the restrictions as designed to protect investors and creditors. Stated limits on purpose and capital appear in the articles of unincorporated joint stock companies, formed wholly at the discretion of private venturers; such examples suggest that investors might want assurance of the boundaries of their commitments and might seek such assurance also when they put their money into corporations. Statutory prescriptions of maximum capital were often accompanied by require-

[50] Cadman, 419, 420; Handlin, 106, 113, 117, 124, 127, 132–33, 161–63, 170, 180; Hartz (1), 40, 41, 62, 76; Hurst (4), 410–12.

[51] Chayes, 36, 37; Hartz (1), 267, 317, 319; Rutledge, 306–8; Stocking and Watkins, 18–19.

ments for minimum capital, which suggest prime concern for creditors. Sometimes mingled with stated limits on capitalization were limits on the voting power of large shareholders, implying that capital structure was the object of investor, as well as general public, attention. These ambiguities of purpose are in the record and should not be ignored.[52] However, there is also sufficient contemporary evidence to indicate that limitations on business purposes, capitalization, and life responded also to the fear that incorporation would help some enterprises upset the market's capacity to function as guarantor of a healthy economic balance of power.[53]

Objections to the business corporation on egalitarian or balance-of-power grounds focused on its social or political significance for the general community and derived from fears of adverse effects upon interests other than those which corporate business immediately served. That legislatures provided incorporation with generosity to substantially all who sought it showed that these fears were far outweighed by practical acceptance of the corporate device as a socially useful instrument of economic growth. But if economic utility were to be the ground of public policy, this rationale itself might invite some regulatory response from law to insure that corporations be so structured, and the behavior of their operators be such, as to realize their productive capabilities.[54] The productive utilities of corporate organization lay mainly in the aid it could give to mustering capital and credit and putting mustered assets under firm central direction. Concern with the functional integrity of the corporation might thus be expected to show itself particularly regarding the relative positions of investors and directors or managers and the protection of creditors.

To some extent nineteenth-century regulatory policy attended to these interests. Yet, in the whole nineteenth century attention to the corporation's ability to fulfill its instrumental utilities seems to have been relatively muted and ambiguous. That more

[52] Berle and Means, 130–31; Cadman, 244; Dodd (8), 269, (16), 812 and (23), 212, 219, 220, 236, 268, 345–46; Livermore, 227.

[53] Note 49, *supra*.

[54] *Cf.* Hurst (3), 218–19, 240, 245.

attention was directed to the external than to the internal or close relations of business corporations stemmed largely from the relative simplicity of most corporate operations up to the late nineteenth century.[55] However, this allocation of policy effort was probably as much accidental as rational. It is consistent with the excessive emphasis from the late eighteenth century into the 1850's on the importance of the sovereign's grant as the basis of corporate status and with the confusion in public discussion in those years between corporate status and special-action franchises. Both factors were calculated to turn attention away from problems of the corporation's functional capabilities to problems of its relations to the general social structure. These appraisals are confirmed when we examine the more self-conscious and elaborate attention given to certain phases of corporation-creditor relations, but particularly to investor-management relations, in the law after the 1890's and notably from the 1930's on. In this later period corporate organization was accepted as a basic utility provided by law to business. But at the same time enormous growth in the scale and complexity of corporate operations directed increasing attention to issues of its functional capacities and the impact of its functional characteristics on the general economy as well as on a broader range of social concerns.[56]

Elaboration of public policy regarding investor, management, and creditor interests belongs to the decades after the 1890's. But we need to recognize some antecedents of such concerns in the earlier nineteenth century. Some mid-century critics joined Adam Smith in the charge that the corporation would impair efficient use of assets because it must depend wholly on agents who could not be expected to display the sustained zeal for profit which moved individual proprietors. But the objection never had visible effect on the growth of chartering, and it disappeared with experience with larger operations.[57] Law in ef-

[55] *Cf.* Berle (1), v; Berle and Means, 131; Dodd (10), 6, 7.

[56] Berle (1), v–vii; Dodd (19), 1008, 1010, 1011; Katz, 179–81, 187, 188.

[57] Adam Smith, 2:229 (bk. V, ch. 1); *cf.* Cadman, 78; Drucker (2), 212, 213; Hammond, 54; Hartz, (1), 57, 58, 60, 69, 70; W. B. Smith, 59.

fect reflected this eclipse as statutes and judge-made doctrine legitimated broad authority in top officers of corporate enterprises and protected this authority with the rule that shareholders might not interfere with regular business decisions of the officers and board of directors or obtain legal redress for alleged mismanagement save upon showing gross negligence or abuse of trust.[58] Legal doctrine thus reflected the rising morale and self-confidence of business management, represented by the railroad executive who in 1886 declared firmly that "private enterprise [that is, old-fashioned individual proprietors] could not manage many of our corporations, and would not if it could." [59]

The best defined respect in which early nineteenth-century corporation law centered on the investor interest concerned the proportionality of shares. Some special charters, notably for banks, limited the number of votes which a shareholder might cast, regardless of the size of his capital contribution. First by judge-made law, later by legislation, stockholders acquired some preemptive right to subscribe upon an offering of additional shares to such amount as would maintain their initial proportion in the corporation's contributed capital. At the outset the preemptive right seemed intended primarily to protect the shareholder's voting position. In this aspect, as in the limits sometimes put on large investors' voting power, preemption emphasized the stockholder's role in the power structure of the organization. Later the rationale of the preemptive right seemed to put more weight on assuring the investor an opportunity to participate in an expanding profitable opportunity, while the disappearance of limits on the voting power of larger capital contributors likewise signaled greater attention to the stockholder's financial interests than to his share of the balance of power. From the 1890's on corporation statutes gave increasing discretion to management to create diverse types of share interests in aid of attracting capital. This development narrowed preemptive rights, which operated only with respect to comparable shares.

[58] Berle and Means, 139, 140, 277, 278; Cadman, 302; Chayes, 34; Dodd (12), 918, 928–30, and (23), 93, 99–101, 141, 191, 193; Stevens (1), 647–51.
[59] Cochran (1), 223.

So, too, did the broader discretion given management to fix
terms of new securities and thus by contract to deny preemptive
rights as incidents of fresh issues. In any event, stipulations on
shareholders' voting and preemptive rights touched relatively
limited aspects of shareholders' interests, compared with the
broad range of financial and operating decisions which might affect the safety and profitability of their investments. These early
nineteenth-century dealings with investor concerns are thus significant mainly because they highlight how far law waited upon
the twentieth century to show broad attention to the investor interest. There was a functional base for this pattern of events.
Railroads and a few large financial institutions apart, business
corporations typically had few stockholders until the end of the
nineteenth century. In these close-held situations investors could
be expected to be knowledgeable enough in affairs to look out
for themselves; many of them would be immediately involved in
the conduct of the firms whose shares they held. Livelier twentieth-century concern with the investor interest followed the increase of corporations with large, dispersed, and less sophisticated bodies of shareholders.[60]

Limited liability of stockholders for debts of the corporation
was a salient utility of the corporate device for enlisting capital.
But the social interest in making productive capital available
touched creditors as well as investors. We put increasing reliance on the market to allocate resources. Security of transactions was a functional requisite of market dealing. Moreover, as
market and technological developments increased social interde-
pendence, there was greater need to make fair and rational adjustments of costs and losses which fell on individuals without
their consent. Both contract and tort claimants had their proper
interests to press relative to the liability of corporate stockholders.

From 1780 to about 1810 the law of corporations showed

[60] On votes: Cadman, 308, 309; Dodd (23), 230, 255, 262, 326. On
preemption: Berle and Means, 133, 144-46, 176-79, 256; Cadman, 256,
257; Dodd (23), 71, 335, 338; Stevens (1), 504; *cf.* Baker and Cary,
829; Rutledge, 330. On the changing investor: Berle (1), v, 2; Berle and
Means, 6; Dodd (10), 12; Hornstein (4), 2:14, 15.

mainly a willingness to give promoters their head. Typically, charters set no conditions protecting creditors; on the other hand, after some initial doubt it became standard doctrine that the silence of a charter conferred limited liability on shareholders. Resort to incorporation was exceptional; ventures which did not succeed seem to have faltered at the outset in these first years; thus there was then no widespread creditor interest to awaken attention.[61] Policy took a different direction as the corporation became available over a wider range of business, especially when men reached beyond the earlier ventures in turnpikes, banking, and insurance to charter corporations for railroads, general industry, and trade. Thus there were no creditor-protection terms in charters for the simple, closely limited enterprises of toll bridges in contrast to the development of restrictive provisions in charters for railroads or textile mills. The first marked concern for the creditor interest took the form of extending only qualified limited liability to shareholders.[62] About mid-nineteenth century legislation took a decided turn toward making unqualified limited liability the norm. But, in evident offset, between 1830 and 1890 statutes created a new set of declared protections for creditors of corporations. The new safeguards accepted that in fact as well as in law money claimants against a corporation were claimants solely upon a separate operating fund. The statutes now sought to assure the economic reality and integrity of that fund by regulating corporate financial operations. There must be a declared capital fund incident to organizing the enterprise; payments must be made into that fund in cash or in property of described character and sound value and not in stockholders' notes; dividends must not be paid out of capital, and if payments were nonetheless made from capital and the corporation thus rendered insolvent, the corporation's directors and officers would be liable to creditors; the corporation might not purchase its own shares if the purchase would impair capital, and apart from statutory limitations some courts ruled that such share purchases were *ultra vires;*

[61] Cooke, 77, 78, 110; Davis, 2:294; Dodd (23), 369–70, 373, 374; Stevens (1), 840, 841; *cf.* Goebel, xii–xxiii.

[62] Note 18, *supra.*

some statutes set a limiting ratio of corporate debt to share-holder investment. That this pattern of financial regulation was a distinctive reaction to the corporation with limited-liability stockholders was indicated by the absence of counterpart regulations for partnerships. In addition to protecting creditors, the new financial regulations could operate in fact to protect stockholders against questionable behavior of management. But the impetus for these developments appears to have been a desire to safeguard creditors, as is indicated particularly by statutory provisions for creditors' suits to enforce the restrictions.[63]

Commentators and courts sometimes summarized the development of creditor protections in the formula that a corporation's capital was a trust fund for creditors. Measured against established limits of equity doctrine, this was a misleading metaphor. Creditors might not proceed in Equity against corporate assets without exhausting their remedy at law, and a creditor had no equitable lien on the property of a solvent corporation. Where Equity did give relief, typically it did so on grounds much more specific than any idea conveyed by the vague image of the trust fund—on the basis that the corporation had violated a statutory duty or was guilty of fraudulent conveyance. The trust-fund metaphor has meaning chiefly in reflecting acceptance by prevailing opinion of the policy of using law to foster production and exchange through multiplying segregated, limited-commitment pools of assets. The main current of policy ran toward promotion rather than toward restriction of economic venture.[64]

It is relevant and economical at this point to anticipate one aspect of the policy developments after 1890 on which the next essay centers. The promotional emphasis was even stronger after 1890 and into the mid-twentieth century, as a new style of general incorporation act gave corporate promoters and top

[63] Berle and Means, 28-31; Cadman, 280, 288; Dodd (7), 31, 32, 35, note 34, 40, 41, 44–46, 48, (8), 268, (21), 1478, and (23), 90, 92–93; Heath, 318; Katz, 181–83; Latty (2), 375; Stevens (1), 841. *Cf.* Baker and Cary, 947, 949; Hornstein (4), 1:13, 2:276.

[64] Berle and Means, 254; Dodd (23), 92; Livermore, 232; Stevens (1), 907, 908.

management more and more power to define and alter the purposes and scale of the enterprise and to shape its financial structure and practices. This freer hand given to corporate insiders was at the expense of the older status of shareholders. But it also materially reduced protections which the previous phase of legislation had purported to give creditors. Statutes now authorized issue of no-par shares or of shares with a low or nominal par or stated value. Thus, stockholders' limited liability might now be coupled with a small starting capital, and—with creditors deprived of such an estoppel-type claim as the trust-fund metaphor had held for them—stockholders' contributions beyond the part declared as capital might be designated as paid-in, or surplus, capital, available for dividends. With majority stockholder approval directors might drastically reduce capital and distribute the resulting surplus or pay dividends from stated capital in partial liquidation. Typically, these capital-reduction powers carried no limits in protection of existing creditors, save for a dubiously useful prohibition against rendering the firm insolvent. Though capital might have been impaired by earlier loss years, dividends might be paid from current or recent earnings. There was a gradual elimination of prescribed ratios of shareholders' contributions to corporation debt. Judge-made law now sanctioned purchase by corporations of their own shares, and legislation did not fully regulate this new authority. Statutes continued to declare some standards protecting corporations' capital funds as a cushion for creditors, but within their general terms and in practice the guarantees worked only against gross abuse.[65]

It is a fair question how much change in substance such changes in law made. Within the framework of formal protection for creditors there was always scope for evasion. There was always room for argument over the value of property given for corporate shares. Individual stockholders were not reliable po-

[65] Baker and Cary, 742, 743, 747-49; Berle (1), 81; Berle and Means, 254; Buchanan, 243–48; Cadman, 277–80, 347, 348; de Capriles, 7–9; Dewing, 1:81; Dodd (8), 274–76, (13), 704–6 and (16), 815; Hornstein (4), 1:128, 326–30, 580, 614, 616, 617; Katz, 181–83; Latty (2), 378–79.

licemen of the firm's finances, whether for their benefit or for creditors' security, for they often had too small a stake to warrant costly lawsuits over alleged watering of stock or dissipation of capital. Usually the law provided no public agency to investigate whether corporations obeyed financial regulations. In the unusual case—as in Massachusetts in certain years—where law charged a public officer with such duties, it gave him no means adequate to the job.[66] The law might have armed creditors better by requiring a full and continuing flow of information on corporate condition, to some public registry. But this is a method of more sophistication than is encountered before mid-twentieth century; the nearest approach to such a development was not by law but by informal pressures from investment bankers and the New York Stock Exchange.[67] The law's failure to stimulate a flow of reliable information on corporate finances was probably more significant than dilution of formal legal safeguards of the corporation's capital. Emphasis on the integrity of the original capital was too static to afford real protection to creditors, whose security depended less on financial origins than on the continuing vitality or want of vitality in the operating enterprise.[68]

The creditor interest accepted the dilution of formal protection accomplished by the trend of corporation law after 1890. Changing business behavior probably explains this acquiescence. The twentieth century saw substantial development in private machinery for credit ratings and credit information, arming creditors to take their own preventive action. Management of established companies grew more prudent, as management interests ran more strongly to maintaining the continuity and market position of firms than to short-run gambles. Moreover, the availability of other legal resources contributed to creditors' acceptance of diminished protections in corporation statutes. Contract law still invited the ingenuity of business lawyers. Where stakes were high enough, supplier creditors and investment bankers

[66] Dodd (7), 32; Hornstein (4), 1:64, 128, 327, 328; Katz, 181; Stevens (1), 859, 863, 864.

[67] Berle and Means, 319, 320.

[68] Buchanan, 247; Stevens (1), 859, 863.

might insist on contractual hedges against financial practice dangerous to their claims. It was customary from early in the nineteenth century for those who lent money to a small, close-held corporation to exact the endorsement of shareholders on the corporation's notes. In dealing with larger firms, creditors wrote into contracts of loan and indentures securing bond issues agreed limitations on dividend policy and capital pay-outs; for the security of advances of materials or goods they learned to use the safeguards of bonded field warehouses.[69]

Federal regulation of corporation financial practices from the mid-1930's on was not an exception to this core policy of leaving major creditors to look out for themselves. True, amended federal bankruptcy laws and federal statutes regulating securities issues—in particular those controlling the structure of public utility holding companies—all applied for the protection of bondholders as well as of stockholders. But the guiding purpose of federal legislation was to protect the new investors who had come into being from the 1920's—numerous, dispersed, often with small holdings, generally lacking information or means to act aggressively for their interests. Along with the broader recruitment of stockholders in the 1920's went a broader market in corporate bonds, creating a body of creditors who in substance were like the new investors in equities—individually weak, lacking knowledge, scattered, and in practice as committed for better or worse to the long-term fortunes of the debtor corporation as were its shareholders. By reviving the idea of limiting the ratio of debt to equity, by providing neutral scrutiny of reorganization plans for distressed corporations, by empowering federal administrators and courts to insist on simplified, understandable securities structures and workable and fair priorities among securities in reorganized companies, the new federal laws protected corporate bondholders along with corporate stockholders. But, measured by practical commitment, this protected class were in substance investors rather than creditors. Moreover, even within the tighter federal regulations, there was manifest preference for keeping the corporate enterprise in exis-

[69] Baker and Cary, 740, 947–49; Berle and Means, 131; Dodd (7), 58; Hornstein (4), 1:326; Krooss, 245; Skilton, 223–25.

tence at the expense—if necessary—of relaxing formal priorities of creditors.[70]

This excursion into policy concerning corporation creditors has gone beyond the 1780–1890 span, which is the principal object of this essay. This period of corporation law policy was rounded out by the standard general incorporation acts, which supplanted special-charter procedures in the 1870's and 1880's. These statutes provided the exclusive means by which business firms might achieve corporate status, and they made incorporation readily available to any lawful business by compliance with simple administrative procedures. These standard acts embodied a considerable residue of regulatory provisions from the previous thirty years of legislative handling of business corporations. This regulation did not deal with elements of the corporation uniquely derived from the state's authority. Most of these provisions stipulated matters which, without the law's command, the ordinary law of contract would have left to the parties' own arrangements—corporate purpose, powers of directors and officers, amendment of articles, share structure, capital requirements, and sources of dividends. Thus, although the standard incorporation acts as these stood in the 1880's involved quite a complex of law-made elements, most of these elements represented not the peculiar gift of the law but a regulatory *quid pro quo* exacted for grant of the entity status which only the law could give. This evolution of policy produced about thirty years of paradox. On the one hand, the corporation statutes now formally adopted a relaxed attitude toward availability of the corporate instrument; it was now made available in a matter-of-fact way as a useful tool of business presenting no value issues other than those of immediate utility. On the other hand, the particular restrictive provisions put into the general incorporation laws stood out as a substantial body of declared regulatory policy in years in which there was otherwise only

[70] Berle and Means, 131; Blum, 584, 586, 591, 602, 603; Dewing, 2:1287, 1315, 1321, 1352, 1361, 1364, 1403, 1414, 1420, 1428; Dodd (4), 784, and (12), 928, 930–31; Drucker (2), 21, 215; Hornstein (4), 1:v, 580; Hurff, 86; Jennings (2), 930, 940; Stevens (1), vii.

limited assertion of regulatory attention to business.[71] Most of these regulatory provisions were of dubious effect. However, the restrictive stipulations in special and general acts did help create in the courts attitudes which for a generation often created a good deal of inflexibility toward problems of corporate powers, with a consequent exaggerated attention to worries over the alleged *ultra vires* character of corporate behavior.[72] However, the apparent equilibrium of policy reached in the standard acts of the 1880's proved short-lived. At the end of the century drastic change set in toward removing regulatory emphasis from the general incorporation acts, with a high premium on giving the greatest freedom and vigor to central management.

[71] Dodd (7), 35, 51, 58; Katz, 181–83; Stimson, 2:9, 10, 14, 21, 22–25, 58–62, 79–80, 87, 91, 96, 100, 117–29, 132–38.

[72] Berle (19), 91, 93; Hornstein (4), 2:26; Rostow (2), 51; Stevens (1), 299, 300, 333.

Chapter II

Legitimacy: Utility and Responsibility
1890–1970

W HAT law permits or accepts, what it enforces or compels, should be socially useful and socially responsible. These have been prime elements in the demand for legitimacy which has been an insistent theme in our legal order. Legitimacy means that no arrangement of relations or of power recognized in law should be treated as an end in itself or as autonomous. An institution must be legitimated by its utility to some chosen end other than its own perpetuation. An institution which wields practical power—which compels men's wills or behavior —must be accountable for its purposes and its performance by criteria not wholly in the control of the institution itself. That legitimacy should derive from utility expresses the pragmatism bred of our experience in opening up a raw continent, through generations in which we were under pressure to improvise and make do with resources frustratingly short of the opportunities. That legitimacy means responsibility—that an institution with power must be accountable to some judgment other than that of the power holders—expresses the prime emphasis this culture puts on the individual as the ultimate measure of institutions.

Utility and responsibility as legitimizers were ideas which materially affected our public policy because they grew out of, and gave form and content to, our experience. However, in proportion as these ideas were not abstractions but living products of our way of life, they embodied the limitations as well as the strengths of our experience. The demand for utility as legitimizer meant that no institutional contrivance should be treated as an end in itself. Yet utility tended to become an end in itself. The utility criterion invited examination of means in relation to ends and hence of the ends themselves. But there was great immediacy of satisfaction in seeing things work, in learning and improving technique, and in counting close-to-hand output. Hence, our experience inclined us to treat operational efficiency or workable operations as establishing the validity of whatever ends they served. Moreover, vested interests of place and profit prompted, or grew out of, particular patterns of operations. Thus means could come to validate ends, or at least induce us to accept uncritically certain ends because we had know-how and immediate interest in achieving them. The other aspect of legitimacy—that power be so structured as to be responsible—expressed tough-fibered judgments bought by hard experience. Weakness in the demand for responsibility did not derive from the immediate context of that demand but from other undesirable by-products of our utilitarian emphasis. Power continually presented new temptations and shifted into new forms. To structure power for responsibility called for continuing, close attention and an investment of resources of mind and energy which we begrudged. We begrudged the investment because we felt that it subtracted from our primary interest in the economy, which was the main area in which we pursued utility. Thus, though the demand to enforce responsibility upon power was real and valid, we were inclined to fumble in realizing it and to fail in will or insight in implementing it.

Between the 1880's and the 1930's developments in both the law and the economy made issues of legitimacy central to the course of public policy concerning the business corporation. The issues that arose in this period had their own cast and urgency. But they were not without earlier analogues.

Before the late nineteenth century questions of legitimacy relating to the business corporation concerned in the main the legitimacy of the ends and means of government's power as it affected corporations, rather than the legitimacy of corporations' use of the facilities the law provided for them. This condition fit the general development of the concept of legitimacy. To the late eighteenth century the concept referred primarily to the power of government as applied to purposes directly pursued by government, with the chief object of limiting abuse of public, rather than of private, power. To legitimate private individual or group economic activity—whether by pressing it toward utility or responsibility—we relied mostly on the market, bulwarked by the law of contract, property, and tort, supplemented by the conventional law of crimes. The presumption of the law was that individual or group economic activity ordinarily required no affirmative license from government; rather, the prime concern for legitimacy was with the legitimacy of using public power to affect private power. This focus of public policy was realistic in a social situation where it was exceptional to find substantial private power based on concentrated assets and disciplined continuity of organization.[1]

What first moved us toward expanding attention from the legitimacy of government operations to the legitimacy of private operations was the multiplication of special-action franchises from the late eighteenth into the first half of the nineteenth century. Concern over legitimacy of such special-action franchises tended to become confused with concern over granting corporate status. Confusion was easy because usually special privileges to establish rights of way and charge tolls or to issue banknotes or to exercise the power of eminent domain—the real objects of contemporary controversy—were given to corporations and were included in the text of the corporate charters. We reconciled such grants with our egalitarian conscience, first, by insisting that government's action must be legitimated by determining that it was in the public interest to confer special privileges to obtain services for public convenience or necessity. Only the legislature might confer such special privileges, and it would do so in a case-by-case scrutiny by special statutes. Second, further to legitimate the government's grants, we began to attach limiting standards, or rules, to the special privileges to protect those who would become dependent on the fairness and quality of the service the franchise holders would provide. Thus, out of initial attention to legitimating the use of the public power, we moved to require legitimacy for private power fostered by law. Next, because important special-action franchises were typically included in corporate charters, it seemed natural to enforce re-

[1] *Cf.* Berle and Means, 353, 356; Dahl and Lindblom, 480–82, 506, 507; Hartz (1), 314–19, and (2), 60, 136, 184, 185; Polanyi, 201, 225, 249, 250, 254.

sponsibility upon the franchise holders by regulating their business organization as well as their business. By the mid-nineteenth century various regulatory provisions—limits on capitalization, for example—became common in special corporate charters and in the first optional general incorporation acts. In what was usually a confused policy debate, demands to regulate special-action franchises moved readily into demands to regulate the franchise to be a corporation, whatever the nature of the business conducted. When all incorporation was put under general statutes at the end of the nineteenth century, the general acts included regulations of corporate structure and procedures. Thus as of the 1880's the standard incorporation acts as well as the rudimentary law of public utilities asserted that organized private power as well as public power must be legitimate. As concepts of legitimacy affected the law of business corporations, businessmen's resort to incorporation affected the concepts of legitimacy.[2]

Concern with legitimacy in terms of both the utility and the responsibility of institutions provided the principal impulse behind the growth of public policy toward the business corporation in the United States after the apparent policy equilibrium of the 1880's. This development was not a neat, explicitly rationalized process. Things have not gone that way in this turbulent, opportunistic society. They did not go that way in the use of the business corporation. Many themes of policy touched the corporation but did not directly spring from attention to its organization or procedures but rather from concern with issues of the federal balance of power, of taxation, of government concern with the business cycle and other aspects of general economic growth. Some impacts of law upon the corporation expressed or reflected not so much rationalized programs as the weight of the law's own institutional inertias or vested interests—for example, incorporation by special statute long after there were any meritorious grounds for this cumbersome procedure. Most of the concern with legitimacy of corporations was implied rather than ex-

[2] *Cf.* Berle (10), 944–46; Brandeis (2), 141–45; Chayes, 34–35; Dodd (20), 557–59; Freund, 40–41, 169–75; Handlin, 99–105, Hartz (1), 69–79; Hurst (4), 175–203, 409–23.

plicit—implied in developing patterns of statutory provisions, court decisions, and the practical use which business promoters, financiers, managers, and lawyers made of the opportunities for contrivance which the law held out or accepted. The record might be easier to read had the most influential public and private policy makers been more given to talk. But the main lines of official and private behavior ran with enough consistency to show that the main values and problems found in using the corporate device centered about its legitimacy.

The utility rather than the responsibility aspect of legitimacy dominated development of public policy toward the business corporation from the late 1880's into the 1930's. We treated the corporate instrument as so useful for desired economic growth as to warrant using law to make it available on terms most responsive to businessmen's needs or wishes. Because we rated its utility so high, we expanded constitutional protection for it against government regulation. Both the utility and the responsibility aspects of legitimacy were in play here, but with significantly different emphases. Acceptance of the corporation's utility was taken to warrant using law to enlarge the maneuverability of private power, while accenting the notion that government regulation of private power should be held to stricter responsibility.[3]

Constitutional doctrine defined both by the United States Supreme Court and by state legislative practice emerged to limit legislation which would subvert the organizational integrity of the business corporation or the functional integrity of the distinct body of assets with which it worked. In doing so, constitutional law and practice respected the corporation as an economic as well as a legal entity. The roots of this policy ran as deep as the substantial use of the corporation for business in the United States. The matter had most dramatic definition in the *Dartmouth College* case in 1819. The New Hampshire legislature undertook to change the governing body of a private chartered college, in effect to convert it into a public institution. Marshall's Court ruled that the statute was invalid because it vio-

[3] Dodd (7), 34–35, and (19), 1008; Eells (1), 200, 201, 287; Katz, 179, 183, 184; McCloskey, 132–34; Rutledge, 338, 340.

lated the clause in the federal Constitution which forbids a state to pass any bill impairing the obligation of contract. To rule that a corporation charter enjoyed the protection of a "contract" under the constitutional provision was a clear-cut act of judicial lawmaking. Indeed, the lawmaking is so clear as to indicate that the Court was pursuing an objective which it rated of high importance. The case did not involve a business corporation. But business corporations were playing a rapidly growing part in the economy, in great measure because their charters gave them operational utilities similar to those which Marshall's opinion noted as making the college an effective, continuing organization. Contemporaries did not emphasize the decision as important for business corporations. But this was, in fact, its prime functional significance.[4]

The decision produced a counterresponse: by special or general statute or by constitutional provision the states came commonly to qualify corporate charters by reserving authority in the legislature to alter, amend, or repeal them. These reserved-power clauses contributed to extend the concept of legitimacy to cover private as well as public power by asserting, as they did, the state's continuing authority to supervise the character of the private corporations it sanctioned. Moreover, the Court acknowledged such reserved powers as of broad effect, though it ruled that the contract clause still forbade a state to take assets, title to which had been vested in a corporation. However, in practice state legislatures were conservative in wielding their reserved powers without the consent of those interested in a corporation. Most matters concerning use of the reserved powers arose in connection with business corporations. Where the reserved power was used in a contested situation, prevailing legislative practice required that good cause in the public interest be shown for amending or repealing a charter. There were instances of highhanded legislative action against particular corpo-

[4] The Trustees of Dartmouth College v. Woodward, 4 Wheaton 518 (U.S. 1819); Angell and Ames, 27, 29, 31, 37; Cadman, 376–79; Dodd (1), 593–95, (20), 559, and (23), 16, 19–26, 28, 41, 126, note 15; Handlin, 151–55; James B. Robbins, 165; Wright, 17–18. *Cf.* Berle and Means, 130, 138, 154, 188, 209, 210; Livermore, 259, note 38.

rations. But these were so rare, usually so hotly contested on appeals to principle, as to show the strength of the prevailing respect for corporate charters. The reservation clauses qualified the impact of the *Dartmouth College* case. But the conservatism with which legislatures used their reserved powers in effect reaffirmed the value which the Court put upon corporate autonomy.[5]

In 1839, in *Bank of Augusta v. Earle,* the Taney Court declared a major limitation upon constitutional protection for the business corporation. In a measured dictum the Court said that a corporation was not a "citizen" within the meaning of the Constitution's guaranty (IV, 2) that the citizens of each state shall be entitled to all privileges and immunities of citizens in the several states. Thus a corporation might not as a matter of constitutional right do business in a state other than that which had chartered it; the other side of this proposition was that a state might altogether exclude a foreign corporation from doing business within its boundaries or might set conditions upon its entry. However, the Court also ruled that it would be presumed that states as a matter of comity recognized the charters granted by their fellow sovereigns, so that a foreign corporation might do business within a state unless it were positively shown that the state's policy was one of exclusion. Federal and state decisions had previously allowed suits by foreign corporations. But the Court now advanced doctrine when it raised the presumption that a foreign corporation might transact legally effective business within the state. In its twin aspects *Bank of Augusta v. Earle* mirrored the tensions of mid-nineteenth-century public policy toward the legitimacy of the corporation. The denial of privileges-and-immunitities-clause protection deferred to that distrust of the corporation which underlay insistence that only a positive act of a sovereign might confer corporate status. On the other hand, the presumption of comity toward the foreign corporation was counterpart of the realities of legislative practice,

[5] Cadman, 94, 95, 96, 379, 380–82; Dodd (1), 586, 599, 610, and (23), 20–21, 28, 29, 32, 41, 141–50, 356, 357; Hartz (1), 238, 240–42, 244, 253; Heath, 314, 315; Hurst (4), 197–204, 207, 420, 560; Livermore, 260; Stevens (1), 577.

which were that in fact almost any businessmen who wanted corporate status could get it. Blurring the outlines of policy toward the corporation here was the issue of federalism; obviously the Court felt that federal judges should be cautious in superseding state with federal models for styles of doing business inside state boundaries. There is at least as much concern for the federal balance as there is concern for the corporation in the policy brew of *Bank of Augusta v. Earle*.[6]

The 1880's and 1890's saw a great expansion of constitutional protection for corporations against state economic regulation. In 1868 the Fourteenth Amendment forbade a state to deprive any "person" of life, "liberty," or "property" without due process of law or to deny any "person" the equal protection of its laws. In 1886 and 1888 the Supreme Court quietly accepted the proposition that a corporation was a "person" within these guarantees.[7] In the 1890's the Court firmly established the principle that corporations might seek protection of "liberty"—freedom to transact business—and of "property"—assets—against unreasonable or discriminatory state laws. In decisions of the mid-twentieth century the Court extended these constitutional protections to "liberty" of speech, press, and petition.[8] In the course of extending Fourteenth Amendment protection to corporations, the Court took much of the substance out of *Bank of Augusta v. Earle*. A state might still wholly exclude a foreign corporation. A state might still impose conditions of entry upon a foreign corporation. But now, if it took the more qualified course, the legitimacy of the regulatory terms it exacted was subject to review by the United States Supreme Court. For the

[6] Henderson, 43–45, 47–49, 56–59, 169.

[7] Waite, C. J., in Santa Clara County v. Southern Pacific Railroad Co., 118 U.S. 394, 396 (1886); H. J. Graham, 566-67. *Cf.* Minneapolis and St. Louis Railroad v. Beckwith, 129 U.S. 26 (1888).

[8] Chicago, Milwaukee & St. Paul Railway Co. v. Minnesota, 134 U.S. 418 (1890); Bell's Gap Railroad v. Pennsylvania, 134 U.S. 232 (1890); Smyth v. Ames, 169 U.S. 466 (1898); Grosjean v. American Press Co., 297 U.S. 233 (1936); Joseph Burstyn, Inc. v. Wilson, 343 U.S. 495 (1952). *Cf.* Allgeyer v. Louisiana, 165 U.S. 578 (1897); Eastern Railroad Presidents Conference v. Noerr Motor Freight, Inc., 365 U.S. 127 (1961). See Walden, 1243.

Court found authority in the Fourteenth Amendment to rule
that a state might be guilty of imposing unconstitutional conditions on entry of a foreign corporation to do local business if
the terms it set were not reasonably or fairly related to matters
of substantial local interest. Moreover, Fourteenth Amendment
due process standards now governed state jurisdiction, apart
from any effort of a state to set conditions on entry to do business. If the state otherwise asserted authority over transactions
involving a foreign corporation, it might be successfully challenged if the Court found that the corporation's activities lacked
ties to local interests or affairs sufficient to warrant the state's
intervention.[9]

To embrace corporations' transactional ability and assets as
"liberty" and "property" of "persons" protected by a substantive reading of the due process and equal protection clauses of
the Fourteenth Amendment was as much an exercise of judicial
lawmaking as it had been to bring a corporation charter within
the contract clause. These readings of the Fourteenth Amendment materially extended the legitimacy which law conferred on
private corporate power and at the same time substantially
curbed the legitimacy of government regulation of corporate behavior. One person reading of these events saw them as the
product of successful conspiracy. The conspiracy theory of the
Fourteenth Amendment was born of innuendo in an argument
by Roscoe Conkling before the Supreme Court in 1882, and
was popularized in ill-defined terms by Charles and Mary Beard
in 1927 in their influential history *The Rise of American Civilization*. According to this melodramatic interpretation, wily
corporation lawyers on the joint congressional committee which
framed the Fourteenth Amendment in 1866, under cover of extending constitutional protection to the newly freed blacks and
other individuals, artfully chose language which would also embrace corporations. Or, at least—for the conspiracy theory was
stated in terms hard to pin down—the amendment's key promoters foresaw that the protected "persons" would include corporations, while the bulk of their naive contemporaries saw only
protection of blacks. The Beards built on the Conkling argu-

[9] Henderson, 134, 143–52, 161–62; Stevens (1), 986–90, 999–1001.

ment of 1882. Conkling invoked general legal usage, which familiarly treated corporations as "persons" for various purposes in law. He claimed support from the journal of the joint congressional committee. His argument pointed, moreover, toward a broad substantive reading of the due process and equal protection guarantees. He pointed out that while the proposed amendment was pending in Congress, there were also pending petitions and bills seeking to protect insurance and railroad corporations from burdensome state laws. Conkling implied that, with federal statutory protection of corporate rights thus on the agenda, sophisticated lawyers in Congress were likely to have intended that the full potential of the proposed amendment's protection of all "persons" in their economic interests be realized, including corporations.[10]

No direct evidence supports this conspiracy theory, either in its extreme or in its milder form. Under close appraisal, the indirect evidence fails to support or actually rebuts the theory. Of course, the law knew corporations as legal "persons" for other purposes—for holding title to land, for example—but this usage in wholly different contexts shows nothing of the intent of the amendment's proponents. Conkling misused the journal of the joint Congressional committee. His argument created the false impression that successive drafts of the proposed amendment in committee enlarged the due process and equal protection guarantees by changing the description of the protected class from *citizens* to *persons*. In fact, *persons* was the word used in all drafts of the amendment and was obviously borrowed from the due process clause of the Fifth Amendment. Contemporary lawyers' usage implicitly refutes the notion that corporation counsel in 1866 would rely on the Fourteenth Amendment to cover their corporate clients—though perhaps less from fear that their clients were not "persons" protected by the amendment than from concern whether the Court would apply the concepts of due process and equal protection substantively to protect businessmen's contracts and assets from unreasonable and discriminatory taxes and regulations. Right up to 1866 and for some time thereafter, skilled lawyers continued—vainly—to seek a

[10] Beard, 2:111–14; H. J. Graham, 38–45; 416–19.

constitutional haven for corporations as "citizens" within the original Constitution's privileges and immunities clause; indeed, this was the basis for insurance company bills pressed on Congress even after the amendment's adoption. Moreover, the contemporary record shows that Congress was cool even to this requested federal protection for corporations; in 1867 the chief lobbyist for the petitioning insurance companies reported only fourteen House members favorable to such federal protection as the companies sought, and none of this little band was a member of the joint committee which produced the text of the Fourteenth Amendment. For nearly a generation before 1866 the arguments of abolitionists and lawyers in slavery and tax controversies had developed the ideas of substantive due process and equal protection. But these arguments had not focused on protection of business associations; the Fourteenth Amendment's due process and equal protection language was simply the staple language of some thirty years of controversy on behalf of individuals.[11]

However, the Fourteenth Amendment spoke in broad standards and not in specific rules. Without violence to language, its protection of "persons" could be extended by fresh lawmaking to cover corporations, and its protection of "liberty" and "property," to cover the functional integrity of corporate business. An important role of constitutional standards is to legitimate adapting legal order to social change. Prevailing opinion accepts such adaptation—particularly at the hands of the Supreme Court—where constitutional doctrine is shaped in conformity with facts recognized as relevant to deeply felt values. No social goal was dearer to the late-nineteenth-century United States than increase of economic productivity. By the 1890's the corporation had emerged as the principal instrument for organizing large business enterprise. Extension of the Fourteenth Amendment's protection to corporations as "persons" provoked no significant contemporary controversy. Within the Court itself there was initial hesitation and some dispute over treating the amendment as imposing broad limiting standards on the substance of state leg-

[11] H. J. Graham, 368, 376, 383, 416–17, 553–54, 558–59, 574, 578, 589.

islation, and from the 1890's into the 1930's there was recurrent sharp criticism of particular trends of decision. But until discussion of the conspiracy theory the focus of dispute was not the inclusion of corporations in the protected class. Nor was there substantial public dispute over reading the amendment to assure some measure of autonomy for business organizations vis-à-vis government. The conspiracy theory of the Fourteenth Amendment flowered into popular dispute long after the relatively unchallenged event, and particularly during the 1930's disenchantment with business leadership.[12]

This late-nineteenth-century development of additional constitutional curbs on state regulation of business corporations represents the negative aspect of the demand for legitimacy in law. Enlarging the policy of the *Dartmouth College* case, the extension of Fourteenth Amendment protection to the corporation put a high social value on considerable autonomy for corporate enterprise.

Implicit in this negative aspect of policy was acceptance of the idea that the law of corporations gained positive legitimacy insofar as it facilitated businessmen's use of the corporation. The years from the 1890's to the 1930's and beyond witnessed a pronounced extension of this positive policy. The standard general incorporation acts of the 1880's made corporate status available through simple administrative procedures for almost any kind of business venture. But these acts offered incorporators a relatively set pattern of corporate organization, subject to various limits on capitalization, share structure, and powers. The courts reinforced this character of the statutes—more rigorously than there was reason to believe legislators intended—by insisting that operations stay strictly within statutory prescriptions. Decisions holding corporate action legally ineffective as *ultra vires* probably did not have broad impact on business behavior, but their threat clouded the conduct of affairs. The first signal of a new trend was in New Jersey in 1888, 1889, and 1893 when legislation authorized one corporation to hold the stock of another. From this beginning, New Jersey, then

[12] H. J. Graham, 26, 558; Haines, 271–78; Warren (2), 2:597–99. *Cf.* Eells (1), 356, 357.

Delaware, and then a number of other states began to offer incorporation on terms of increasing liberality. By the 1930's a new type of general incorporation act had emerged throughout the country. The new statutes provided a standard corporate structure but allowed it to be varied within a range of increasing generosity by such departures as draftsmen might put into the corporation's articles or bylaws; the common formula either defined a structure which should obtain except as the articles or bylaws might otherwise provide or simply committed certain elements of structure to the will of those conducting the enterprise. The acts of the 1880's had ratified the dominant practice of the preceding century by accepting corporate status as a matter-of-fact instrument. But these acts retained traces of earlier distrust of the device by continuing to insist that incorporators accept significant limitations of corporate structure. The movement of policy from the 1890's into the 1930's carried the utilitarian attitude about as far as it could go: if the law of corporate organization was legitimated by its utility to business enterprise, legitimacy would be most fully achieved if the law empowered businessmen to create whatever arrangements they found most serviceable.[13]

The new style of corporation statutes in effect judged that corporate status had no social relevance save as a device legitimized by its utility to promote business. The obverse of this judgment was that regulation of business activity was no longer to be deemed a proper function of the law of corporate organization. The function of corporation law was to enable businessmen to act, not to police their action.[14] In practice, the function of the new style of corporation law was yet more specific. In proportion as the laws relaxed or abandoned limits which the 1880's-type statutes had imposed in behalf of investors, creditors, and general social interests, they legitimized control by the active insiders—promoters, entrepreneurs, top management—

---

[13] de Capriles, 4, 5, 13–14; Dodd (7), 35, 51; Hornstein (4), 1:189; Katz, 179–81, 187, 188; Latty (3), 596, 601–2, 612; O'Neal, 1:127–28; Rutledge, 337; Stevens (1), 6, 24.

[14] Berle (3), 1049; de Capriles, 13–14; Dodd (3), 1145; Latty (3), 601–2.

who would wield the authority to draw up the corporate articles and bylaws, fix the share structure, and decide on financial policy. In substance through the new pattern of corporation acts prevailing opinion accepted the proposition that the legitimacy of corporation law lay simply in serving vigorous promotional will in developing and consolidating business enterprise.[15]

Diverse interests and attitudes supplied the dynamics of the movement of policy from the standard of the 1880's—in which the law on the whole set the structure of the corporation, while making this law-fixed device generally available—to the standard of the 1930's—in which the law sanctioned such corporate organization as private draftsmen chose to create. Despite the importance of the subject, there is no abundance of direct evidence to identify the prime movers. The historian confronts here a problem of scarce sources familiar to the student of legal history. Until the federal securities legislation of the 1930's, almost all lawmaking about the organization of business corporations was done by state legislatures and state courts. Unlike the comparative riches supplied by the published records of congressional hearings, committee work, and debates, state legislative records are typically a bare-bones collection. The press usually finds little that is newsworthy in what goes on at state capitols, in contrast to the range of attention it focuses on the Hill and the White House. Where important values are enmeshed in technical detail, there is little likelihood that the moving forces will be reflected in unofficial published papers. To a considerable extent we must identify interests and pressures and their resolutions by inference from the formal decisions taken by legislatures and courts.[16]

Prime movers in the first drive toward the enabling type of corporation statute were two interests of narrow focus and questionable social value. Civil War financing instructed the first generation of investment bankers in the United States and helped develop the first broad investment market. The rapid

[15] Berle (3), 1050, 1067; Berle and Means, 127, 130–31, 247, 279, 287; Dodd (8), 273, 275, (12), 918, 928–30, and (19), 1006–8; Benjamin Harris, 15–16; Latty (3), 596; Rutledge, 338–40.

[16] *Cf.* Hurst (3), 12–13, 168–78, and (4), x–xii.

growth of railroad empires after 1870 showed the possibilities of a larger scale of business organization than the economy had known before. At the same time the railroad boom showed the possibilities of profit in manipulating more elaborate arrays of equity and debt securities than the stock or bonds which enterprisers had ever before contrived. By the 1890's new technologies and the promise of larger markets sustained by a fast-growing population were spurring development of large industrial firms outside the railroad field. Men concerned with profit from financial maneuvering saw expanded possibilities for themselves in this course of events if they could shape corporate organizations to their needs. Back of the generous powers which New Jersey and Delaware were willing to confer on corporate entrepreneurs were the pressures of a relatively small force of financial venturers and their lawyers. Symbol of the self-styled responsible leadership of this interest was J. P. Morgan. Morgan perceived an expanding market for limited-commitment investments in a growing upper middle class of increasing affluence and in the financial intermediaries—insurance companies and banks—on which this class relied. Morgan needed a larger stock in trade—corporate shares and bonds—to realize the potentials of this market. To some degree he also saw the need to maintain investing confidence in this broader market. Confidence meant that the investment banker should use his strategic command of capital to police against unsettling competiton; entry to industrial markets should be barred to rash newcomers, and those already in should be persuaded or pressured to accept reasonably stabilized market shares. This investment banker's approach put first priority on a corporate structure which allowed creation of large aggregations of capital and centralized inside control of corporation finances—both to take advantage of the investment market and to determine the conditions of change and stability.[17] This demand found willing cooperation in

[17] Allen, 70–80; Berle (8), 211; Cochran (1), 35, 50–51, 70–73, 102, 108, and (3), 155–56; Hacker, 195, 211, 213–14, 216, 230–34, 410–12; Hornstein (4), 1:66, note 14; Johnson and Krooss, 293, 305–7, 312–13, 319–21; Sutton et al., 248–50.

the states which pioneered in the new type of corporation acts. These states competed for the fees and taxes they could have for charters and from the companies they chartered. The possibilities were enhanced by the late nineteenth century because of the new protections of the Fourteenth Amendment, under which corporations could now operate outside the states from which they had their charters. In the first enthusiasm for liberalizing the corporation laws, about half a dozen states staked out their competitive claims. However, New Jersey and Delaware stayed far ahead of the field—and continued to do so into the second half of the twentieth century—in part because they held out their favors with such generosity, in part because their courts gave sympathetic treatment to the new laws, in part because they were convenient to the financial and industrial heartland. Delaware and New Jersey charters especially provided the legal framework for large-scale enterprise.[18]

By the 1930's what had begun as competitive chartering in a handful of states had set a national pattern of corporation law. By then in most states of commercial, industrial, or financial importance the available incorporation statute was an enabling act, offering to those organizing or controlling a corporation broad scope to arrange its structure to their design. In the 1960's this pattern continued as the norm.[19]

This movement of policy became too general and showed too much staying power to be explained simply as the product of the states' competition for fees and taxes or of the ambitions of a tight circle of bankers and promoters whose horizons extended simply to financial maneuver. Investment banker influence declined, relative to the command over assets possessed by big corporation management through retained earnings and by financial intermediaries of a new scale and weight.[20] Common adoption of the liberalized corporation statutes blunted the

[18] Allen, 75; Brandeis (1), 559, note 37; Hornstein (4), 1:64, 71, 74, 80, 81–86; Stevens (1), 6.

[19] Berle (3), 1049; Dodd (7); 51; Katz, 179–81.

[20] Goldsmith, 139, 140, 142, 144, 145, 148, 160; Kuznets, 57; Krooss, 224, 225; Lerner, 301; Redlich, 2:360; Sidney Robbins, 33.

states' competition for fees and taxes. And the common availability of corporate status under the new acts meant that they provided the organizational frame for the general run of incorporated firms and not only for those which sought a special haven state for their special ends.[21]

The generality of the new policy pattern implied some broader value base than that which underlay the beginnings in the 1890's. As the narrower launching impetus may be symbolized by the elder Morgan, the broader—and more durable—base of policy seems grounded in quite different attitudes represented by Morgan's contemporary, Andrew Carnegie. True, Carnegie himself did not put a high value on the corporate device. He was contemptuous of financial manipulations effected through corporate mergers and the attendant manufacture of corporate securities. He resisted incorporation of his own steel works because he desired to keep decision making tightly centralized in a limited partnership whose members he as general partner chose and which his will and energy dominated. But Carnegie stood for an approach to business which the new style of corporation statute could serve. Carnegie saw the mission and the profits of business, not in financial maneuver, but in production regularly increased and made more profitable by investing in the best methods that developing technology and managerial skills could devise. Moreover, he held before him the vision of constantly expanding markets, which he would command by hard-driving competition in quality and price supported by technical and managerial efficiency. The promise of lasting growth and gain Carnegie saw, not in materials or money, but in large-scale organization; organization was the new factor of production.[22] As the country moved into an expanding economy through the 1920's, prevailing opinion shared this faith in the key importance of energy and skill in business direction. The new corporation acts—designed to allow full

[21] Hornstein (4) 1:iv, 14, 66, 69, 70, 72; Jennings (1), 194–96, 206; Rutledge, 311; Stevens (1), 980.

[22] Cochran and Miller, 182, 194–202; Hacker, 4, 342, 344, 345, 347, 348–50, 351, 356, 358, 360, 365, 366, 387, 392, 398, 413.

scope to vigorous policy direction and management at the center—were consistent in structure with this faith in the productivity of such organization.[23]

Broad adoption of the enabling-act type of corporation statute appeared to show a new equilibrium of public policy. In one respect appearance matched reality. From the 1930's through the 1960's no effective demand developed to return to more restrictive terms of incorporation.[24] The late 1930's heard some renewed talk of requiring federal charters for firms in interstate business, to enforce federal standards of corporate organization and practice. But the idea never rallied enough support to become a serious candidate for Congress's attention.[25] Thus, it seemed established that we would not henceforth use the grant of corporate status as leverage for regulating any considerable range of business behavior. Apparently we were prepared to treat the corporate instrument as raising no questions of social values, except for the judgment that it was legitimated by its utility in promoting enterprise and that for that use it should be available freely and substantially on such terms as enterprisers found most serviceable to their ends.

However, this agreed frame of policy was too narrow to contain all the important issues of social order which the wide and varied use of the business corporation presented. Interest conflicts which generated increasing concern in the mid-twentieth century showed that the utilitarian theme which dominated policy development from the 1890's into the 1920's was not alone sufficient to legitimate the corporation. Various changes in both statute and judge-made law sounded afresh the theme of the responsibility of power. But now the theme was of the responsibility of private, rather than of public, power. Concern for responsibility had never been wholly absent, but it had been far subor-

[23] Berle (20), 18; Drucker (2), 212, 213, (3), 5, 27, 37, and (4), 3; Eells (1) 48, 301–3, 356, 357; Means, 156–58; Sutton et al., 22, 34–36, 358, 387. *Cf.* Cooke, 79; Weber, 157.

[24] de Capriles, 4, 5; Eells (1), 71, 74, 141, 148, 152; Latty (3), 596, 601–2, 612.

[25] Dodd, (12), 930; Loss, 1:107–11; Rutledge, 340.

dinated around the turn of the century. More insistent questions now pressed for answers. Utility was not enough. We must ask, utility for whom and to what ends? [26]

Concern with the responsibility of private power wielded within business corporations arose at both ends of the range of enterprise, small and large. Different kinds of tension existed according to the size of firms. But the various issues all raised fresh questions of legitimacy. Corporations whose shares were held within a small, close circle and not traded on any general market presented the danger that majority shareholders would oppress the minority. Corporations with sizable numbers of shareholders, whose shares were traded in some general market, presented the danger that minority shareholders or management insiders would oppress the majority.[27] A few hundred of the largest business corporations, moreover, achieved a degree of economic power in the market and possessed such capacity to affect the well-being of their labor, suppliers, and customers and the general interest that the legitimacy of their power must be measured by reference to values outside those of their own institutional being.[28]

Both the set-pattern incorporation acts, which were standard as of the 1880's, and the enabling-act type of statute, which became standard by the 1930's, tacitly assumed that the corporation would be one with a substantial number of shareholders. This bias was perhaps natural, since such had been the character of the enterprises prominent in the controversies and produced by the most active pressures out of which corporation law evolved. The record shows no significant attention given before the mid-twentieth century to the question whether a different corporate pattern might be more suited to the needs of a firm with relatively few investors, most of whom would usually be in continuing touch with its affairs, if not actively involved in operating it. Yet, in fact, as the corporate form came into wider use in the late nineteenth century and in the twentieth century,

[26] *Cf.* Sutton et al., 22, 255–56; Williams, 401–4.

[27] Dodd (7), 35, 58; Hetherington, 130; Latty (3), 603; Stevens (1), 591.

[28] Berle (11), chs. II, III.

most corporations were of small or modest capitalization with few stockholders. Many corporations were continuations of firms which had been one-man enterprises or partnerships; many conducted business which in most respects could be as well handled in unincorporated form.[29] What such businessmen wanted was to operate with the flexibility, informality, and close control of their affairs which characterized one-man ownership or a partnership and at the same time to enjoy certain advantages either distinctive to the corporation or most handily achieved through it. Limited liability of shareholders for firm debts was probably not the dominant inducement one might assume it to be. This was an important protection against tort claimants, though insurance could supply much protection, also. On the other hand, substantial creditors were likely to insist that the small corporation's notes be backed by the personal endorsement of its stockholders. However, incorporation still offered continuity for the enterprise against the death or withdrawal of any particular participant and provided a convenient, standardized form within which to relate investors who were more involved, and those who chose to be less involved, in operations.[30]

But the standard pattern offered even by the liberalized incorporation statutes was in important respects dysfunctional for the close-held firm. A lesser problem was that the standard corporate organization contemplated rather formal procedures in operations—regular election of directors, regular meetings of the board, keeping minutes, and formal proposals and votes on business. The close-held firm had incurable tendencies toward informality; meetings were not held, elections were omitted, minutes were not kept. Informality raised no problems so long as all were content, but it became threatening if there were conflict within the firm or with outsiders.[31]

The more difficult problems which the standard form of in-

[29] Berle (1), v; Evans 4, 5, 45, 47; Hurst (4), 413, 414.
[30] Baker and Cary, 16–18; Hornstein (3), 441, and (4), 1:3, 190; Hurst (4), 414; Kramer, 433; Livermore, 2, note 2; *cf.* Stevens (1), 11, 12.
[31] Hornstein (4), 1:399; O'Neal, 1:160, 161.

corporation posed for the close-held firm concerned control. A minority investor in a close-held corporation was peculiarly vulnerable vis-à-vis the majority. The discontented shareholder in a firm with a sizable number of shares outstanding could usually find a market for his interest; even if an unhappy minority did not sell out, the possibility that it might could put some curb on majority action. In the close-held situation, especially where business policy was in controversy, no outsider was likely to buy in; the minority's only market was likely to be the majority. Thus individuals investing in a close-held firm had reason to write into its organization requirements of unanimity or specially high requirements for a quorum or a deciding vote on critical matters, along with stipulations against dilution of their relative voting power. Again, the stockholder in a firm of many shareholders usually had no involvement with the enterprise other than as a claimant on dividends. But to many an investor the close-held firm provided a job, and even if he did not rely on the firm for a salary, participation in its affairs might be an important return on his investment. The standard incorporation acts were not responsive to these interests. Under them the corporation was run by a board of directors to which the law ordinarily committed substantial autonomy vis-à-vis the stockholders; where stockholder votes counted, a majority vote was usually determinative. Implicit in this pattern was the judgment that investors who wanted full control of their business should be content with a partnership. But what many businessmen wanted was in effect an incorporated partnership.[32]

Until well into the twentieth century there was little specific legislative response to the organizational problems peculiar to close-held corporations.[33] With insistent energy businessmen and lawyers concerned with greater power for promoters and managers in large enterprises pushed through the liberalization which began in New Jersey and Delaware. In contrast, no sustained pressure from business or bar appeared to adapt the stat-

[32] Baker and Cary, 16–18; Hornstein (4), 1:v, 189, 190, 546, 603, 606; O'Neal, 1:119–21, 127–28, 191; Stevens (1), 10, 11, 566, 591.
[33] Kessler, 720, 721; Latty (3), 600, 601; Stevens (2), 483, 491.

utes to the small firm.[34] True, the type of corporation act which became common by the 1930's, with the broad discretion it gave private draftsmen, allowed lawyers to frame articles and bylaws to suit the close-held firm. To some extent lawyers used this new freedom, but it was by no means common. Inertia, laziness, and want of imagination undoubtedly figured. But a proper caution on the part of lawyers may have been a large factor, in view of policy attitudes taken by the courts.[35]

Late-nineteenth- and early-twentieth-century decisions generally refused effect to agreements of shareholders to pool their votes or to require unanimity on basic matters, arguing that each participant was entitled to the independent judgment of each of his fellows and to the benefits of majority rule. Courts also refused effect to corporate articles which conditioned board action on stockholders' consent or which by classifying shares sought to guarantee particular shareholders fixed representation on the board. From the standard terms of the general incorporation acts, judges concluded that public policy required that effective command of all regular business be in the board of directors and that the board not be structured to represent segmental interests among investors. Such positions made sense for corporations with many stockholders. In such companies there was need of a board so constituted and with such autonomy that it could be charged to act for the best interests of the whole body of shareholders and against the threat of control for the benefit of a few insiders. But in close-held corporations the prime danger was that the majority would oppress the minority. Moreover, there was reason to believe that shareholder agreements expressed true shareholder interests in close-held firms; in contrast, among numerous, dispersed stockholders forms of agreement might only conceal the hand of inside manipulation. Nonetheless, until well into the twentieth century, courts, even in states of the most business sophistication, would not recognize that different functional problems between close-held and

34 de Capriles, 5, 6; Hornstein (4), 1:v, 190.
35 de Capriles, 5, 6; Hornstein (3), 441; Kramer, 434; O'Neal 127–28.

broadly held corporations called for different policies. By the mid-twentieth century there was a cautious trend in the decisions to give effect to stockholder agreements requiring unanimity, or at least more than majority concurrence, on some corporate actions. But it was a limited movement, and it left matters in much uncertainty.[36]

Efforts to qualify the ordinary authority of the board of directors awakened the peculiar hostility of the courts. This reaction —which otherwise seems out of proportion to any public interest that might be thought at stake—perhaps reflected the high value which prevailing opinion put on the entrepreneurial function in the growth decades from about 1870 to the 1930's depression.[37] That it was a threat to effective, concentrated management which was specially suspect may be implied from more tolerant judicial reactions to some other draftsmen's devices dealing with problems of close-held corporations. So, for example, despite a strong tradition hostile to restraints on free transfer of property, twentieth-century courts were willing to accept certain agreed limitations on transfer of shares where the restraint might serve the continuity and working harmony of the enterprise.[38] Again, courts would accept a good deal of informality in close-held operations; where practice implied the parties' agreement to waive votes or official meetings or the like, judges would often find grounds in ratification or estoppel to uphold corporate action.[39]

In most respects, however, the courts' acknowledgment of the special circumstances of close-held firms was not an adequate substitute for forthright statutory legitimation of distinctive treatment of such corporations. To leave matters to the hazards of litigation introduced a good deal of uncertainty in business arrangements.[40] Yet, if courts were hesitant or sometimes

[36] Hornstein (3), 441, 443–45, and (4), 1:189, 190; Kramer, 434; O'Neal, 1:207, 230, 236; Rutledge, 328, 331, 337, 338–40; Stevens (1), 10, 11.

[37] *Cf.* Allen, 111, 114, 138; Drucker (4), 4–5; Prothro, 44, 55–57, 86, 210, 223–24; Sutton et al., 65–66, 93.

[38] Hornstein (3), 445, and (4), 1:248, 249; O'Neal, 2:4, 12, 14.

[39] Hornstein (4), 1:399, 506–8, 635; *cf.* Kessler, 719.

[40] Hornstein (3), 441; Kessler, 719; Kramer, 434; Stevens (1), 10.

seemed rigid in their views of policy, the judges could plead want of legislative guidance. The first statutes plainly designed to meet some of the special problems of close-held corporations only appeared at mid-twentieth century in North Carolina and New York. These acts centered on the issue of investor control of management. They legitimated the corporation's agreement to buy its own shares. They allowed stockholders' voting agreements and irrevocable proxies to implement such agreements. They sanctioned election of the board by stockholder class voting, removal of directors by stockholders, restrictions on board discretion and particular powers, and election and removal of corporate officers by the stockholders. They permitted stipulations for high quorum and voting requirements for board action, though they also allowed provision for a board quorum of one. They accepted informal action to the extent of authorizing stockholders to act by unanimous written consent without a meeting.[41]

Compared with private arrangements which came to the courts over several decades earlier, this legislation contained little that was new. The novelty lay in statutory legitimization of the various elements. The most striking aspect of the matter was that so much time had to pass to obtain this sensible clarification, and then only in a few states. The fact attested to the difficulty of putting legislatures into motion without the push of an energetic lobby. There is no evidence that legislation was wanting because legislators shared strongly the institutional conservatism which had led courts to deny effect to special arrangements for the close-held firm.

Despite this show of legislative interest, no state enacted an incorporation statute to deal with the close-held corporation as such.[42] The same inertia and absence of focused interest-group pressure which delayed more specific legislation militated against a comprehensive response to the problems. Wider use of the corporation in business was, by mid-twentieth century,

[41] de Capriles, 5; Henn, 442, 444; Hornstein (4), 1:190, 204–6, 1954 Pocket Part, 54–57; Latty (3), 600, 601; O'Neal, 1:198, 199.

[42] de Capriles, 5; Hetherington, 92; Hornstein (4), 1:204; Rutledge, 328, 331, 337, 338–40.

awakening fresh concern with the legitimacy of the private power which the corporate form helped into being. However, our nineteenth-century legacy identified the issue of legitimacy with the big corporation. Hence we lagged in perceiving that more extended use of the corporate instrument in smaller enterprise generated problems of legitimacy special to that use.

A different set of issues of the legitimacy of private corporate power emerged after 1890 out of the activities of big business. The great trunk-line railroad stood for a time alone as the exemplar of a new scale of business entity, carrying such practical power as to require particular legitimation. The public policy response through a specialized law of public utilities suggested that the problem was peculiar to one type of economic activity. As first the trust, then the holding company, then a wave of turn-of-the-century mergers spread large-scale organization into wider reaches of the economy, public policy was slow to acknowledge that broad new issues of legitimacy were posed, beyond the scope of older formulas. We entered this new era with two principal means to assure the legitimacy of private economic power. Prime reliance was upon a competitive market, the discipline of which would curb waste, excessive ambition, oppressive charges, and disregard of productive service. Within the framework of market discipline, we relied on the self-interested care of those who put their capital at risk to police the fidelity and efficiency of the policy making and management of particular firms. Symbols of the dependence on the legitimizing function of the market were the Sherman Act ban on monopolies or combinations in restraint of trade (1890) and the standards in the Clayton Act and the Federal Trade Commission Act (1914) aimed at preventing growth of private power which might ripen into restraint. Symbolic of the dependence on the legitimizing function—within the firm—of the investor's profit-oriented scrutiny of management was the Michigan Supreme Court's ruling in 1919 in *Dodge Brothers v. Ford Motor Company:* management's prime obligation was to pursue profit in the interests of shareholders and not to adopt pricing policies designed to promote the interests of wage earners or to effect wider sharing of the gains of improved technology.[43]

Surging change in the economy after the 1890's in large part undermined confidence in these foundations of legitimacy. By mid-twentieth century about five hundred large corporations dominated large sectors of trade and industry in the United States. Firms of their size no longer operated under the impersonal discipline of the kind of market whose existence had been an assumption of public policy concerning business organization —a market in which participants were numerous enough and modest and equal enough in resources for no one or several to control price and quality competition by overt collusion or by mutually regardful business policies. In the sectors in which such large firms moved, three to eight firms now commonly accounted for the bulk of trade. In this situation it appeared that the terms of competition could be substantially managed, without collusion, by the reciprocal regard which a few dominant firms had for each other's action. With large capital commitments and fixed charges, big companies in this kind of market seemed especially inclined to limit price competition. They sought growth but gave highest priority to maintaining relative market position and protecting such a flow of earnings as would secure their continuity. The classical market held management to a criterion of short-term profits, which, however many social values it ignored or unduly subordinated, was quite definite and exacting. The new market might allow management opportunity for a wider choice and ordering of goals. What the realities were was a matter of sharp debate among economists. But, in any event, the appearances of the new situation inevitably invited questions about what external criteria should now measure the social utility of power wielded by those controlling such corporations.[44]

[43] 26 Stat. 209 (1890); 38 Stat. 717, 730 (1914); Dodge v. Ford Motor Co., 204 Mich. 459, 170 N.W. 668 (1919). *Cf.* Dorfman, 3:21–26; Hurst (2), 81–82, 91–94; Nevins and Hill, 88–105.

[44] Heflebower, 110–16; Kaysen and Turner, 26–41; Mason (1), 45, 50, 52, 54, 347–50.

The apparent decline of old-style market discipline might be taken to cast a heavier burden on the law to deal directly with the legitimacy of the leadership of corporations. Moreover, the rise of big business posed corollary questions of the legitimacy of corporation law, as well as of the private power wielded within the structures which corporation law sanctioned. We cannot neatly measure the influence of corporation law on the changes which put in question the capacity of the market to discipline private business power. But, at the least, corporation law developed in ways which reinforced financial, entrepreneurial, and technological pressures for an economy of large firms. By the early twentieth century legislatures were commonly removing statutory limits on corporate capitalization and purposes.[45] Authorization of holding companies provided a ready instrument for increasing the size of business operations under central command: the holding company allowed pyramiding of voting power so that limited, but strategically concentrated, resources could control large but diffusely held assets.[46] By authorizing new types of investment—in no-par stock, varieties of preferred stock, and varieties of debt instruments—more liberal corporation laws helped promoters appeal to a broader and more diverse investing public.[47] Other developments in corporation law encouraged the trend toward bigness by strengthening or consolidating the relative autonomy of those holding both formal and informal central control of corporate policy.[48] This factor had the further effect of helping alter the other traditional pillar of corporation legitimacy, the supervising role of the stockholder. We now need to take a look at that aspect of the matter. Of course, it took development of business skill and invention to realize on the possibilities which law thus afforded for a larger

[45] Dodd (7), 32, 36, 38, 40, 41; Hornstein (4), 1:134.

[46] Berle (5), iv, v, (8), 211, and (14), 112; Berle and Means, 203–6; Buchanan, 318–23; Chandler (2), 30, 31; Dewing, 2:1040–45; Dodd (7), 30, and (8), 274, 275; Hornstein (4), 1:26, 125.

[47] Berle and Means, 75, 135, 141, 143, 148, 185, 186, 268; Dewing, 1:68, note e, and 2:984, 985; Dodd (8), 273–75, 278, (10), 6, 7, 8, and (23), 269; Knauss, 624; Kuznets, 56, 57.

[48] Berle and Means, 138–52; Dodd (7), 35, 43, 51, and (12), 928–30; Hornstein (4), 1:64, 67, 78.

scale of firm. But such changes in law did facilitate release of business energy, if they were not indeed indispensable to it.

The conventional view assigned the stockholder two roles in legitimating corporate power. His interest in a share of the corporation's earnings defined a primary goal of the enterprise; satisfaction of that interest was—in law as it was assumed to be in fact—the key measure of management's performance. Stockholders were also to play an active role—and in some respects the superior role—in the internal governance of the corporation; their votes elected the board of directors, and on some basic matters decisions of the board must often have the assent of a majority or more than a majority of the shareholders. In both respects, the shareholders' involvement would insure that those immediately in charge of the enterprise would be held to a profit-seeking performance, which under market discipline would make the firm an acceptably productive contributor to the economy.[49]

For the company with few shareholders, this characterization was likely to have reality. In proportion as the number of shareholders rose, however, the proportion of fiction grew. By midtwentieth century, even modest-sized firms among those providing the bulk of production and trade counted their shareholders by the hundreds or thousands. In this context business fact and corporation law combined in effect to require radical redefinition of the stockholder's relevance to the legitimacy of private power.

The stockholder's legitimating role was probably never as the legend would have it, in those cases where a sizable body of shareholders pooled assets to create a large enterprise of complex operations. Nicholas Biddle ran the Second Bank of the United States through tight inside control, while the generality of the bank's shareholders acquiesced. In the second half of the nineteenth century the great railroad—the original model of the large industrial corporation—was invariably the creation of

[49] Allen, 70–71, 235–36; Angell and Ames, 562; Berle and Means, 132, 135; Bowen, 126–28, 132; Carnegie, 2:808; Cochran (1), 92, 93; Drucker (1), 76–77; Schumpeter (2), 66–67, 71–72; note 43, *supra.* But *cf.* Handlin, 158; Hartz (1) 75.

some strong, closely centered leadership, which set objectives and made decisions quite free of influence from most stockholders. A determining factor was size; in big firms the practical pressures and opportunities for insider autonomy produced similar results in the nineteenth and twentieth centuries.[50] On the other hand, the character of investors shifted in the twentieth century in directions which peculiarly reinforced the withdrawal of stockholders from such superintendence as would legitimate those in fact controlling large corporations. Investment in corporate debt and equity securities was still relatively uncommon into the late nineteenth century; in December 1886 issues listed on the New York Stock Exchange included only sixty railroads, four express companies, nine miscellaneous corporations, and seventeen inactive stocks, and altogether the array included shares of less than a dozen industrial corporations. Investors in corporate shares were likely to be businessmen looking for outlets for their surplus earnings, who, while attracted by the limited-commitment opportunities which the corporate form allowed, had an entrepreneur's concern with the profit possibilities and records of the companies into which they put money.[51] In contrast, as the roster of corporate shareholders rapidly expanded from 1900—especially in the 1920's and after World War II—more and more investors were salaried, wage-earning, and professional people, whose concern was not with short-term profit but with assured income and long-term appreciation. This was not an entrepreneurial-minded style of investment. Those of this mind were even less likely than their nineteenth-century predecessors to measure corporation management by short-term profits or to care to spend time or energy in close scrutiny of corporate operations.[52]

[50] Allen, 71; Cochran (1), 121–23, 219–20; Handlin, 158; Hartz (1), 75; Hurff, 4, 5; Redlich, 1:60; W. B. Smith, 37, 247, 248.

[51] Cochran (2), 345, 350, 354, 382 (comment by Williamson); Davis, 2:294; Dodd (10), 7, 8, and (12), 928; Gregg, 120, 130, 131, 137; Johnson and Krooss, 306–7, 312, Knauss, 624; Sobel, 130–31; Wohl, 153.

[52] Allen, 236; Berle (14), 32, 36, 45, (11), 30–32, (16), 18; Berle and Means, 66–67, 121, 285; Johnson and Krooss, 320; Livingston, 22–32; Manning (3), 261; Reagan, 142; Sobel, 158–59, 182, 237–42, 252–55.

Still another change in investment practice affected the place of shareholders in the governance of large corporations. Through the mid-twentieth century increasing millions of individuals invested in corporate securities at second remove by buying life and casualty insurance, creating trusts in care of bank trust departments, purchasing mutual fund shares, and becoming participants in industrial pension funds set up through collective bargaining. By the 1960's the great institutional investors were the largest buyers of corporation bonds and, in response to a steady march of inflation, became substantial buyers of stock. As the number of institutional investors increased, some prophets said that these investors, moved by their stakes and informed by their expertise, would begin to play in earnest the supervisory roles of the legendary stockholder. But through the 1960's the record showed little to bear out the prophecies. The size of their assets commanded respect when institutional investors sought information; by their probing they introduced some fresh surveillance into corporate affairs. Nonetheless, the institutional investors generally behaved as individuals did; like individuals, they expressed dissatisfaction with the government of a corporation by selling out rather than by voting their shares for new men or different decisions. On rare occasions institutional investors cast their weight for a change in top management; rarer was evidence of their influence brought to bear on particular issues of corporation policy. This abdication of the stockholder's supervisory role perhaps derived from traditions of trusteeship; institutional investors were trustees, and fiduciary standards dictate that the trustee should not by his own decisions put the assets in his charge at business risk. A more powerful restraining influence was implied in the rapid increase in the size of such institutional holdings. These stakes gave opportunity and occasion for intervening in the affairs of the corporation whose shares were held, but they also carried a heavy moral, and in some outcomes perhaps a legal, responsibility for exercising such control as the shareholding might allow. Already under responsibility to those for whose benefit they held shares, professional fund managers did not seem anxious to incur further responsibility to their fellow shareholders in the companies in which they invested. At bottom, the position seemed unstable. Institutional investors' demand pressed hard on the supply of corporate securities. As their holdings became larger relative to supply, the possibility loomed that they might find themselves unable to resolve their dissatisfactions with corporate performance by selling out, lest they so dislocate the shares market as to cause unacceptable capital losses. Thus, weakness bred from the strength of their investment positions might force them to be active rather than passive shareholders. But as of the 1960's such a development was speculative. Meanwhile the relative passivity of these big investors underlined the general failure of shareholding to supply the steady surveillance by which stockholders were supposed to legitimate the power wielded in business corporations.[53]

The increasing number of investors who sought gain or security from limited commitments spelled the failure of stockholders to fulfill their formal roles in the internal government of large business corporations. However, developments in the law of corporate organization contributed materially to this outcome.

Three elements were critical if shareholders were to perform some substantial role in enforcing responsibility upon the immediate controllers of a large corporation. Shareholders needed information on the conduct of the corporation's affairs. They needed voting power to act on their information. They needed leverage in law by which as individuals or as a small group they could get action for the benefit of the enterprise against the inertia or contrary interest of the controllers or the indifference of the generality of shareholders. The standard pattern of corporation law in the states by the 1880's made sufficient provision for shareholders under these headings to give some substance to their supervisory role, though their endowment did not put them

[53] Berle (14), 43–45, 54–57; Baum and Stiles, 35, 41; Goldsmith 140, 142,; Benjamin Graham, 221; Kuznets, 57, 58; Lintner, 193, 194; Livingston, 35, 57, 98, 133–45, 212, 216–18; New York *Times,* Feb. 27, 1964, 41:2; Sobel, 182–83, 349. On limitations of trusteeship: Scott, 3:1816–17. On obligations of "control": Berle (13), 1222–23; Dodd (10), 13; Hornstein (4), 1:472–75; Stevens (1), 567–74.

in a position to act with vigor and dispatch. The prevailing trend of state law from about 1890 to 1930 did not improve, and in some respects weakened, the stockholders' capacity for effective oversight. The span from the 1930's through the 1960's included more active concern in law for the shareholders' power position than any previous era had witnessed, but there were strong enough crosscurrents to deny a clear net gain in stockholder impact. In view of the fact that stockholder surveillance was the principal internal factor on which tradition relied to legitimate corporate power, this inconclusive record is puzzling—unless we interpret it to evidence how deeply prevailing opinion valued, or at least accepted, management autonomy as legitimating corporate power by its utility in advancing economic action.[54]

As firms grew larger, with more complicated problems of finance and production and with more shareholders, the ordinary stockholder had more need of reliable information about its affairs and more difficulty in getting it without positive help from the law. The circumstances which made information essential if there was to be some substance in the stockholders' supervisory role also made a monopoly of information a potent factor in building the autonomy of those in immediate control.

State law offered two approaches to the matter—by declaring some right in the stockholder to examine the corporation's books and by requiring periodic reports by the corporation to its shareholders. Of the two, the reporting requirement offered the greater potential for strengthening the stockholders' role; it required positive action by management. To see the books the shareholder might have to fight and win a lawsuit. Moreover, required reports could be used to exact explanations from the knowledgeable insiders, while effective inspection of the books might call for precisely that sophistication in the company's affairs which stockholders lacked and could not readily supply. But the course of state policy did not follow these realities. Consistently through the nineteenth and into the mid-twentieth century, states failed to impose effective reporting requirements in

[54] Berle (3), 1050, 1067; Dodd (7), 34, 43, 49, 51, (10), 9, 12, 38–41, 45, and (16), 815, 817; Katz, 179–81; Rutledge, 327–33.

their corporation laws. Many required no regular reports at all to shareholders or to any public officer. Those which required some reports usually asked only for meager information, commonly made no requirement of reports from subsidiaries, and provided no effective enforcement of the modest demands they laid down. State tax laws somewhat increased the reporting of corporate financial affairs but not to such an extent as materially to change the weak pattern of state policy. As late as 1965 a count showed that among the fifty states and the District of Columbia, twenty-two jurisdictions had corporation-report requirements of some type; in only fourteen of these twenty-two were reports available to stockholders, and in three the requirement might be dispensed with by the corporation's bylaws. Only two states required certification by a public accountant, and generally there were no specific stipulations as to the content of reports.[55] In contrast, the course of state policy concerning access to corporate records was somewhat more favorable to the stockholder. Judge-made law early and consistently recognized some such rights in shareholders. However, the courts imposed limitations which invited contests—the shareholder must seek access to the books in good faith (that is, strictly in his role as shareholder) and for proper purposes—and this was probably the stockholder right most often in litigation over the years. By the late nineteenth century statutes commonly reinforced the common law right of inspection, and following the legislative lead the courts tended to interpret the statutes liberally in favor of the shareholder. The fact remained, however, that this approach put considerable burdens of initiative and often battle upon the shareholder, and to be effective it was likely in practice to require that he already possess the kind of inside knowledge he was seeking.[56]

It is consistent with the emphasis of public policy on making the corporation a ready instrument of vigorous central manage-

[55] Cadman, 319; Dodd (6), 206, and (10), 44, 45; Hornstein (4), 2:127; Livermore, 142, 234; Loss, 2:825, 826; Knauss, 625; Manning (1), 1486; Rutledge, 333.

[56] Cadman, 320; Dodd (10), 40; Hornstein (4), 2:123–28; Rutledge, 331, 333; *cf.* Dewing, 1:98, 99; Gower (2), 1380, 1381.

ment that, when we produced some regulations which fostered a significant flow of information to stockholders, we did so back-handedly. The really effective pressures for stockholder information grew out of concern for maintaining confidence in the market for corporate securities rather than for the legitimacy of the internal government of corporations. It is indicative of the original bias of policy that the most effective pressure began with the late-nineteenth-century expansion of the listing requirements of the New York Stock Exchange. The Exchange moved from the first request for some reports from listed companies in 1866 to a strong suggestion for the filing of annual reports in 1895, to a requirement of annual earnings reports and submission of balance sheets in 1900, to a 1909 requirement that listed companies distribute annual financial reports to their stockholders, and then to an active threat of delisting to enforce requirements of annual reports in 1932 and to enforce a minimum of informative detail in 1933. Overlapping this general trend was the development of various Exchange rulings against market manipulation by the management of listed companies, mainly by extending information requirements, for example, requiring prompt announcement of dividends and stock dividends and splits. It was probably not accidental that this effective pressure for stockholder information came from a single central agency—albeit an unofficial one—asserting power in a national market. The Exchange was not under the competitive pressures which after the 1890's encouraged states to drop strong regulatory provisions from their corporation laws.[57]

Policy followed this same channel when in 1933 and 1934 the first major direct legal action to bring more information on corporate affairs to shareholders came from the federal government. The Securities Act of 1933 imposed disclosure requirements regarding original issues. In the ensuing generation these requirements proved generally adequate and workable, and by them the Securities and Exchange Commission exacted a compliance which exposed this category of corporate decision making to a public accountability unmatched in state law. The 1934

[57] Berle and Means, 293, 294; Hornstein (4), 1:150, 186, 334, 335; Livingston, 157–59, 161, 163–66; Loss, 2:804–8, 1179.

Securities and Exchange Act requirements of disclosure affecting listed securities worked to provide a large new flow of information, though under less rigorous demands and with less administrative scrutiny than marked the regulation of original issues.[58] Apart from its direct impact, the SEC operated within its statutory framework to promote two important ancillary sources of stockholder information. The SEC had statutory authority directly to regulate company reports only under the Public Utility Holding Company Act (1935) and the Investment Company Act (1940). But it was inventive in fostering broad disclosure through the general run of company reports to stockholders. Thus, by a 1942 rule a report to stockholders which satisfied SEC requirements would be accepted to satisfy annual reporting requirements under the Securities and Exchange Act. In 1954 the SEC annual report form under that statute was amended to require that the SEC be furnished, by the date on which the document was first sent to stockholders, any annual report which a regulated company made to its stockholders for the registrant's last fiscal year; since the company would hesitate to allow discrepancies to appear with its required reports to the SEC, this filing requirement applied substantial pressure in policing the scope and reliability of what was sent the shareholders.[59] The SEC applied a second auxiliary pressure by promoting audits of company statements by independent accountants. The SEC had no statutory authority to prescribe a uniform system of accounting as such. On the other hand, it was authorized to prescribe accounting standards relevant to enforcing the statutes it administered. It used this authority vigorously in setting forms for preparation of financial statements required, for example, in connection with registration of new issues or solicitation of proxies. The SEC did some innovating. But on the whole its contribution was to put its weight back of the best standards advanced by accountants themselves and to insist on conditions of audit which increased the outside accountant's independence vis-à-vis his client. By the 1960's qualified opinion

[58] Berle (16), 19; Dean, 697–99, 702, 704; Hacker and Zahler, 423–24; Heller, 758, 759; Knauss, 646, 647.

[59] Loss, 1:348, 349.

was that the SEC's influence had worked great improvement in corporation accounting practice. Again, as with the strengthening of stock exchange listing rules, a sharp contrast emerges between the regulatory weakness of state corporation law and the positive impact of action taken by a national professional group backed by national law.[60]

His right to vote—to select the board of directors and perhaps to consent to basic changes in the nature of the enterprise —was the element in the stockholder's legal status which made him essential to the internal constitutional structure of the corporation; it was by his vote that he would formally confer legitimacy on the power wielded by those immediately controlling the firm. The legislative record in effect acknowledged that a factor fundamental to the social acceptability of the corporation was involved here. Despite the dominant trend of the statutes after 1890 to enlarge the freedom of the central controllers of corporation action, no legislation committed the determination of stockholder voting rights completely to the draftsmen of corporate articles.[61] Within this framework, however, the post-1890's legislation and practice under it whittled away at shareholder voting power. One approach was to allow the corporate articles to elaborate the share structure so that full voting rights rested in but one class of stock; others might be declared non-voting shares or assigned limited voting rights, as when a preferred stockholder was entitled to vote only after some specified default in dividends. Another approach was to put wide discretion in a simple majority of shares—which in a firm of large, diffused shareholding would be rather readily subject to the lead given by the controllers—to effect mergers and other basic changes in the character of the enterprise. There were some crosscurrents; thus statutes might provide rights for dissenting stockholders to receive an appraised value for their shares upon

[60] Dean, 745–46; Dewing, 1:532, 533, 535; Dodd (14), 176, 177, (17), 1258, (18), 268; Hornstein (4), 2:14, 15; Knauss, 630–31; Loss, 1:333, 341, 347, 350. *Cf.* Berle (16), 19, and (17), 430; Berle and Means, 310, 312; Dodd (19), 1008, 1010.

[61] Hornstein (4), 1:400, 483–84; Manning (1), 1493, 1494; Rutledge, 327, 328, 330; Rostow (1), 33–34.

a merger. But by the mid-twentieth century the state corporation laws gave broad discretion in financial policy to those in
control and, in particular, commonly approved creation of non-
voting shares and other limited-participation shares.[62] The principal opposing policy came from the same sources which
worked to strengthen the flow of information to stockholders.
By refusing listing, the New York Stock Exchange put a substantial curb on creation of nonvoting shares. And in particular
areas of business—under the Public Utility Holding Company
Act and the Investment Company Act and with reference to any
corporation which sought reorganization under new federal
bankruptcy procedures—Congress in the 1930's and 1940's out-
lawed nonvoting shares and provided for strengthening the
claims of shares of limited voting rights.[63]

As events developed, however, the core reality of stockholder
suffrage in the big company lay in the use of the proxy machinery. The common law said that a stockholder might not
name an agent to exercise his vote. But from an early point special statutory charters authorized proxy voting, and by the mid-
nineteenth century it was firmly established legislative policy.[64]
Originally a device for the convenience of the shareholder, the
proxy became indispensable to mustering a substantial number
of votes when rosters of shareholders grew to large size. Given
the advantages of the corporation's purse, their near monopoly
of knowledge of its affairs, and the almost total absence of limitations in state law on what they might initiate and what they
must tell, the controlling men at the center of a big enterprise
moved into full command of the proxy machinery. By the
1930's the proxy, which had begun as a convenience to the
shareholder, had become the principal instrument for insuring

[62] Baker and Cary, 324, 325; Berle (7), 251; Berle and Means, 75–
76, 132, 135, 139, 141, 148; Dodd (12), 920, 921, (16), 815, 816, and
(23), 192, 193; Hornstein (4), 1:186, 400–401; Katz, 185–86; Rohrlich,
207.

[63] Baker and Cary, 324, 325; Berle and Means, 76; Katz, 185–86;
Rohrlich, 208.

[64] Berle and Means, 139; Cadman, 305; Dodd (23), 227, 311, 326;
Hartz (1), 255, 256; Hornstein (4), 1:186, 421; *cf.* Handlin, 158; Hartz
(1), 75; Livermore, 229; Manne (1), 407.

that the stockholder voting majority, which legitimated management, was almost always at the disposal of management.[65] The Securities and Exchange Act of 1934 and the exercise by the SEC of its rule-making authority under that act constituted the principal and most effective response in public policy to these facts. Here, as generally, the SEC emphasized disclosure as the prime instrument to hold private power to useful and responsible roles. By requiring that management's proxy solicitations state clearly the purposes for which proxies were asked, supply material information on nominees for the board of directors, set out executive salaries and other compensation, and furnish an adequate financial statement, the SEC probably did as much as could be done by improving the flow of information to make stockholder votes potentially more effective in the government of the large corporation. After extensive hearings in 1956 the SEC extended its regulations explicitly to require comparable disclosure by those soliciting proxies in opposition to those presently in control.[66] The SEC's statutory authority was not limited to requiring disclosure. Thus the SEC also required that management include in materials accompanying proxy solicitations proposals submitted by stockholders or provide reasonable opportunity for stockholders to convey proposals directly to their fellows. In practice the stockholder-proposal opportunity was little used and had little success; less than 5 per cent of proxy statements filed annually with the SEC contained any stockholder proposals, and such proposals as were made almost uniformly failed of adoption. The development of the stockholder-proposal rules was less significant for any material impact on corporate organization and policy than for what it further revealed of the high social value still being put on fostering and protecting the utility of the corporation as an instrument of sus-

[65] Aranow and Einhorn, 259, 492–94, 508–14; Baum and Stiles, 12; Berle (11), 180 and (14), 105; Berle and Means, 86–88; Dodd (12), 918, 919; Garrett, 312–17; Hornstein (4), 1:428; Livingston, 19, 39–42; *cf.* Redlich, 1:60; W. B. Smith, 247, 248.

[66] Baker and Cary, 210, 211; Caplin, 666, 667; de Capriles, 13, 14; Dean, 737–39; Garrett, 315, 321, 322; Hornstein (4), 1:429–32; Loss, 2:866, 868, 1027–36; Manne (4), 115; Manning (3), 229; von Mehren and McCarroll, 730, 736, 737.

tained, vigorous economic operations, deriving effectiveness from a substantial autonomy. Thus the SEC declared that the stockholder might not use the proxy machinery to advance proposals for corporation stands on matters of general public policy not integral to its business operations; or for proposals not proper for stockholder action under the law of the chartering state; or for proposals to redress personal claims or grievances or to decide a matter of ordinary business. Also a proposal could not be repeatedly advanced unless it obtained increasing support at the rate of at least 3, 6, and 10 per cent of the vote in successive years.[67]

As their combined pressures produced fuller regular reporting by corporations to shareholders, the SEC and the New York Stock Exchange both worked toward broader availability of the proxy channel for stockholder expression. Some corporations did not solicit proxies. The SEC did not use its rule-making authority to require that companies solicit proxies, though it discussed a modified form of the idea with a congressional committee in 1957. However, in 1955 the New York Stock Exchange required all newly listed companies to agree to do so. By 1959 the Exchange could report that less than 3 per cent of active listed companies did not solicit proxies, and it put all listed companies under threat of delisting if they were not seeking proxies by 1961.[68]

Federal regulation of the proxy machinery produced, as an important by-product, a greater flow of information on corporate affairs. There was reason to believe that, because of the requirements of publicity, managements sometimes refrained from, or altered, courses of action they might have pursued in more privacy.[69] But the record did not show that the federal-proxy regulation substantially increased stockholders' participation in the internal governance of large firms. Management normally nominated the only individuals who stood for election to

[67] Aranow and Einhorn, 255–60; Bayne et al., 413–18, 427; Bazelon, 191; Caplin, 671, 672; Gower (2), 1392, 1393; Hornstein (4), 1:432, 433, 453; Loss, 2:900–909, 911; von Mehren and McCarroll, 736–39.

[68] Dean, 737; Gower (2), 1392; Loss, 2:1027–36.

[69] Caplin, 667; von Mehren and McCarroll, 739.

the board of directors, and management normally defined such other business—including the initiation and shaping of proposals for mergers, executive compensation, and other key issues of policy—as proxy forms put to stockholder vote. Encouraged by the favoring federal laws and appealing to concern about the legitimacy of managements more and more obviously separated from control of the general body of shareholders, spokesmen for an ideal of shareholder democracy won some prominence in the second quarter of the twentieth century. Under the testing of twenty years or more, this movement failed to develop a coherent theory of corporation law or operations and failed to make any significant mark on the substance of big-company goals or operations. The most tangible accomplishments of the movement were to make management more aware and more adept at the polite forms of relations with shareholders. Indicative was the limited range of matters for which men used the stockholder-proposal opportunity created by the SEC proxy rules, as well as the almost total want of success in obtaining adoption of any of the propositions advanced.[70] The shareholders' most practical opportunity for a determining role arose when an organized group, contesting for control of the firm, solicited proxies in opposition to the management slate. Such contests continued to be rare; even in the more hospitable environment of the federal proxy regulations, less than 1 per cent of corporations with shares listed on organized exchanges were involved in proxy fights annually.[71] The big corporation remained typically a one-party system of private government under management direction, given formal legitimacy but no great difference of substance by the more strictly policed proxy machinery.

That the general body of stockholders proved in practice unable to use its votes to confer substantive, and not merely formal, legitimacy on the controlling power in large corporations did

[70] Bazelon, 191; de Capriles, 13, 14; Emerson and Latcham, 69, 112, 113, 141; Garrett, 315, 317–23, 336; Hornstein (4), 1:431, 432, 433; Manne (2), 1443, and (4), 115; Manning (1), 1487; Rostow (2), 54–56, 70–71. But *cf.* Manne (1), 407–10.

[71] Garrett, 317–23; Hornstein (4), 1:431. But *cf.* Manne (1), 411–13.

not show that there was no possible role for the stockholder. Though ineffective as a body, stockholders as individuals might operate as a check-and-balance force within the enterprise—through lawsuits or through the stock market.

Directors and officers owed to shareholders duties of loyalty and of care. Until the federal securities legislation of the 1930's statute law contributed relatively little to developing these standards. To the 1880's the regulatory provisions in corporation statutes expressed more concern for creditors and for protecting the market against corporate power. To the 1880's, insofar as the corporation statutes looked to protecting the shareholder, the protection was mainly by defining his commitment to the enterprise—in limiting definitions of purposes, capitalization, and share structure—and because limits were absolutely stated, there was a tendency to believe that within the statutory authorizations those in control had unchecked power.[72] When a major shift began in the statutes from the 1890's on, the change in effect put so high a social valuation on vigorous central management that the new legislation gave little guidance toward standards restrictive upon the controllers. It was the courts which developed a body of doctrine demanding fidelity and care of directors and officers. Probably because corporate affairs were relatively simple at first, the judge-made law did not begin to emerge until near mid-nineteenth century. Its main development waited upon an increase in scale and complexity of corporate business from about the turn of the century. Decisions laid down obligations of good faith (avoidance of conflict of interest) in strict terms and generally enforced the standards as strictly as they were stated. There was in practice less substance to the strong words in which judges declared the duty of due care which rested on directors and officers. Sensitive to their lack of business expertise and confronted by the generosity with which post-1890's legislation endowed corporation management, the courts imposed a difficult burden of proof on complaining shareholders to prove misconduct or negligence—and not merely mistakes of business judgment—as the necessary basis of redress. Too, those in control used the broad authority

[72] Berle and Means, 134–35; Dodd (23), 70–71.

the statutes gave them to restrict stockholder rights by contract, with limiting terms written into the corporation's securities.[73] Over-all, however, the trend of judge-made doctrine was to tighten the standards of behavior required of those effectively holding corporate power. From the 1920's on, this direction of policy was made most evident as decisions extended the obligations of good faith and care to embrace not only those formally charged with the immediate governance of the firm—directors and officers—but individuals or groups who in fact wielded control of the enterprise.[74]

Standards of fidelity and care were not enough. To fulfill the criterion of legitimacy someone other than those subject to the standards should be available to enforce them. Through the 1960's we continued generally to commit this responsibility to individual stockholders. In a showdown they could apply their force only by suing the faithless or careless directors, officers, or other controllers. To fashion a remedy here called forth some of the most striking policy creativity shown by judges in the field of corporation law. When the shareholder's complaint was not of some wrong peculiar to him but of wrongful conduct of the enterprise as a working entity, question arose of his standing. Almost as early as businessmen began making considerable use of the corporation, Equity responded by giving standing to the shareholder, not in his own right, but as complainant for the corporate interest. Since the plaintiff's standing was derivative —arising from the corporate interest and not from an interest peculiar to him—the suit was a representative suit, and any recovery must go to the corporation and not to the plaintiff.[75] The corporation might itself sue for wrongs done by those con-

---

[73] Berle (1), 189, (3), 1050, 1067, 1074, (4), 1367, 1371, 1372, and (17), 429; Berle and Means, 221, 227–29, 275–76; Dodd (3), 1145, (4), 782–84, (10), 37–46, (12), 925–27, (16), 814, (19), 1006, 1007; Hornstein (4), 1:527, 530, 531, 541; Katz, 179; Stevens (1), vii, 567–74; Timberg, 566–70. *Cf.* de Capriles, 13–14; Dodd (19), 1008.

[74] Berle (13), 1212, 1214, 1215, 1217–24; Berle and Means, 234, 245; Dodd (10), 13; Hornstein (4), 1:472–82; Stevens (1), 568. *Cf.* de Capriles, 13; Manne (4), 116, 117.

[75] Gower (2), 1385; Hornstein (4), 1:vi, 2:96, 99, 103, 191, 205; Rostow (2), 48.

trolling it. But in practice such actions would be brought only after a change in management. Thus the stockholder's derivative suit proved to be the main reliance for enforcing the responsibilities of corporate power holders.[76]

Experience showed that the stockholder's derivative suit was a device of limited utility. Shareholders were handicapped for want of facts. Litigation costs ran high, and it was difficult to muster fellows to share the costs. Judicial doctrine made management subject to standards of good faith and care, but these were generalities which for impact must be reduced to specifics by hard contest over the particular context in which the behavior complained of had gone on; thus added to the out-of-pocket costs of a complex litigation were all the costs of delay and uncertainty of outcome. Since recovery would go to the corporation treasury, there was typically little incentive of direct interest to sustain the plaintiffs if they were honest men. There was also real danger of encouraging lawsuits brought simply to induce the corporation to buy a settlement.[77]

Doctrinal limitations added to the practical difficulties of the stockholder's derivative action. Some judge-made, and later some statute, law limited such suits to plaintiffs who owned their shares at the time of the transactions of which they complained. In 1944 the New York legislature, responding to an aggressive lobby for management interests, required that, unless the plaintiffs represented a substantial percentage or dollar value of shares, they post bond for the costs and expenses of defendant directors or officers; this barrier was too high for most potential complainants to surmount. Several other states followed the New York example. In another favoring of management over stockholders, legislatures shortened the period of the statute of limitations on such actions, even though shareholders

[76] Berle (4), 1367, 1371–72, (17), 430, and (18), 437; de Capriles, 15; Dodd (10), 39, 42, 43, and (17), 1263, 1264; Hornstein (4), 2:205, 258, 259; Rostow (2), 48, 49. But *cf.* Manne (4), 113.

[77] Berle (16), 18 and (17), 430; Dodd (7), 51, (10), 39–41, and (12), 925, 926; Hornstein (4), 1:vi, 2:102, 103, 205–6, 217, 218, 223, 224, 226–27, 257–58; Livingston, 51; Rostow (2), 49; Rutledge, 331–33; Stevens (1), vii, 827.

needed time to overcome their usual problems in obtaining information and mustering means to challenge those in control. Other statutes at mid-twentieth century authorized corporations to reimburse directors and officers for outlays in defending stockholders' suits, usually without the safeguard of requiring that defendants succeed on the merits of the dispute or that the court approve such settlement as they might have made.[78]

In any event, apart from creation of statutory handicaps to the plaintiffs and favors to the defendants, the record showed a low level of success of derivative actions. Availability of this remedy was commonly counted the most potent sanction the stockholder had. But, in context, this judgment said more of the weakness in the corporate scheme of checks and balances than of the utility of the derivative action.[79]

Where there existed a broad, active market for a corporation's shares, the investor held a continuing power to vote approval or disapproval of the firm's conduct by buying in or selling out. Inherently, this power existed only in respect to companies of substantial assets with sizable numbers of shareholders. Inherently, it was a power of limited range; it enabled the investor to give an over-all approval or disapproval but not to pass judgment on particular policy while remaining in the enterprise. Within these limits, however, share trading might give investors considerable practical power to consolidate the position of existing management on a rising market or to render management vulnerable to a take-over by rivals who could afford to buy a controlling interest in a falling market. Given the demonstrated flabbiness of the stockholder electorate and the severe legal and practical handicaps on the individual stockholder suitor, by mid-twentieth century the investor's resort to the stock market might seem the most effective base for assigning him a role in legitimating corporate power. This view is made plausible by

[78] de Capriles, 15, 16, 17; Dodd (17), 1263; Frampton, 326, 333–39; Hornstein (1), 123, and (2), 1; Jennings (1), 199–205; Katz, 184; Livingston, 48, 49, 51.

[79] Berle (16), 19; Dodd (9), 226, and (15), 140; Hornstein (1), 123 and (4), 2:257, 258; Manne (4), 113; *cf.* Gower (2), 1385, 1387–89. But *cf.* note 76, *supra.*

well-publicized take-overs or take-over battles. But it must be rated as largely speculative, so long as no one has inventoried the relation which the publicized cases bear to a broad range of management histories over a substantial time. Without such an inventory, it seems equally plausible to judge that take-overs helped by a falling shares market were too episodic or extreme to represent a major role for investors in legitimating corporate power.[80]

If the stockholder had most effect on corporation policy through the stock market, this fact would fit the main trend of public policy since the 1890's, which had been to use corporation law to foster management autonomy and to develop controls on corporate power outside the law pertaining directly to corporate organization. However, the law's relations to the investor and the securities markets present considerable ambiguity of purpose. From the early twentieth century there was a spread of state legislation (blue-sky laws) to protect investors in corporate securities, until almost every state had some such statute on its books. The bulk of these sought only to ban fraudulent promotions; a minority provided administrative scrutiny of the soundness of the issuers' financial structure; almost all suffered for want of adequate provision for enforcement.[81] Congress provided Interstate Commerce Commission regulation of the issue of railroad securities in 1920, and it launched a broad reach of federal regulation of issuing and trading in securities of the most important business corporations in the national economy with the Securities Act of 1933 and the Securities and Exchange Act of 1934.[82] These state and federal laws directly regulated corporate organization insofar as they fixed standards for defining the financial structure of enterprises. To some ex-

[80] Opinions giving weight to the stockholder's market "out": Chayes, 40, 41–45; Director, 23, 24; Lindblom and Dahl, 284–85; Livingston, 33, 89, 143; Manne (4), 113, 114, 115, (2), 1433, 1444, and (3), 548, 549; Sidney Robbins, 33. But cf. Baker and Cary, 223; Berle (11), 180, and (14), 105; Dodd (12), 928; Emerson and Latcham, 69, 70, 102, 112, 113, 141; Livingston, 38–42, 51, 135.

[81] Jennings (1), 208–29; Loss, 1:23–31, 33–43, 57, 58, 90, 93; cf. Berle (18), 434; Berle and Means, 303–9, 319–20; Loss, 1:31, 3:1432, 1433, 1435.

[82] Baker and Cary, 937–39; Berle (9), 237, (16), 19, (18), 435;

tent such regulation—especially the federal regulation—indirectly regulated management conduct apart from securities issues; thus disclosure requirements might dissuade the controllers from certain operating decisions which they would not want to expose to controversy. However, most of the regulatory attention went not to mustering new capital but to protecting the integrity of trading in securities already issued and to guarding security holders' claims on corporate earnings.[83]

Particularly from the 1930's on, the record showed a lively development of public policy concern with investors in corporate securities. But, on the one hand, experience amply testified to the fact that this concern was not realistic if it depended on investors to be active, vigilant critics of management. On the other hand, as corporations ranging from substantial to very large size preempted the bulk of production, commerce, and finance; as their needs and ambitions generated a great increase in the supply of investment shares and debt instruments; as an increasingly affluent population sought outlets for savings and reliable flows of income corollary to its regular earnings; and as more and more families invested directly in the stock market or indirectly through institutional investors of rapidly mounting size, a social interest arose in the investor quite different from the original concern with him as a part of the internal governance of the firms whose shares he held. This new social interest was an interest in the corporate security structure as a whole, as a now essential part of the machinery for distributing income and wealth, maintaining broad, reliable, consumer purchasing power, and bulwarking the life expectations of millions of individuals with such assurance as contributed not only to economic but also to political stability.[84]

Viewed in this perspective, the law's increasingly active atten-

---

Dean, 697–706, 747; Dodd (10), 12, and (12), 930–46; Gower (2), 1375; Heller, 758, 759, 768–71; Jennings (2), 930, 932, 936–38, 940; Knauss, 613–15, 646, 647; Loss, 1:vii, 8, 123–25, 186, 325, 348–50, 3:1435, 1444.

[83] Berle (8), 212; Loss, 1:277. *Cf.* Caplin, 667; Dodd (5), 248; Fleischer, 1148, 1150, 1151; Knauss, 647; Loss, 1:186, 277, 325; von Mehren and McCarroll, 739.

[84] Berle (14), 50, 52, 54, (18), 441, 446–48, and (20), 13, 15; Chayes, 28; Drucker, (1), 87; Eells (1), 258; Harbrecht, 280–82, 285,

tion to investors in the mid-twentieth century belonged less to the legal history of the business corporation than to the legal history of the social organization of wealth and income. The distinction may clarify the dynamics of public policy—the felt pressures that gave it direction and force. Thus the distinction helps explain why there was a great growth of legal regulation on securities trading and aspects of corporation finance touching the reliability of flows of income from corporate securities in mid-course of a span of years when otherwise the law lent all its favors to management's autonomy and showed little effective concern with the stockholder as a participant in corporate government. Moreover, the distinction in policy goals made a difference in the law's impact. Much of the regulatory content of corporation statutes into the 1880's protected the investor in ways which implied that his social utility was that of one who bore risk and pressed the firm to seek maximum profit in the short-run terms of a price-competitive market; hence we find statutory provisions protecting the limits of the investor's commitment—restrictions on the firm's purposes, capitalization, and share structure—and judge-made law enjoining directors and officers to make the stockholder's gain their guiding measure. The regulatory content of the 1930-70 laws for the investor aimed at a regular, secure flow of returns and assurance against insiders' maneuvers which might imperil continuity of the enterprise and its reserve strength.[85] Measured by nineteenth-century entrepreneurial concepts of the investor's goals, mid-twentieth-century regulation was likely to be satisfied by more modest achievement. Perhaps underlying was a fresh question of the stockholder's own legitimacy as it had earlier been conceived; if he was typically a passive recipient of income and of relatively modest capital gains from steady growth, he should not claim from law the kind of concern which it might show for a more active and responsible participant in corporate power.[86]

287; Knauss, 614, 615; Knauth, 147, 158–59; Loss, 1:21, 22; Reagan, 79; Shaw, 163. *Cf.* Baum and Stiles, 29–32; Berle and Pederson, 176; Cooke, 82; Loss, 1:111; Stevens (1), 621–27. But *cf.* Adler and Kelso, 210; Manne (3), 614, 615.

[85] See note 82, *supra*.

[86] Berle (11), 30–32, 180, and (18), 449; Chandler (2), 314, 322; Chayes, 40; Dahl and Lindblom, 258, 284–85; Drucker (3), 340, 342;

There were those—both within corporations and outside of them—who argued at mid-twentieth century that top management was developing a working character which in itself legitimated the power resident in large corporations. The argument rested largely on the significance of expertise, institutional procedures, and continuity in the existence of the big firms. Large corporations performed productive functions on which society was critically dependent; the key importance of the functions made their fulfillment self-legitimating. The big firms' operations demanded more specialized administrative and technical skills than in days of simpler business; functional need thus tended to bring to the top a professional style of leadership. Their operations required pooling diverse skills and sharing risks of decision where stakes were high; thus corporation government by committee grew and with it an inclination to make judgments according to what would foster the growth and security of the firm as an institution. Normally commanding the proxy machinery from their central position and bulwarked by the corporation's treasury, chief executives and boards of directors controlled the designation of leadership; their own continuity strengthened their tendency to make corporation policy by whatever broad balancing of factors would promote the continuity of the firm. The combination of such factors was seen as encouraging a climate of corporate statesmanship. Statesmanship in corporation decision making meant fidelity to the productive function coupled with readiness to seek fair adjustment among all major elements closely affected by what the big company did —not only its shareholders but its workers, suppliers, dealers, and customers—and to be a good citizen in its relations to the general community.[87] This approach was not inconsistent with profit seeking, either in ideal or, according to some evidence, in practice. However, it was an approach which did not seek the

---

Livingston, 13, 19, 32, 39, 62–63, 71, 87, 193; Loss, 1:13, 19; Manning (1), 1490, 1491, (2), 42, and (3), 261; Maurer, 167, 187; Reagan, 142; Rostow (2), 54–56, 70–71; Sutton et al., 61, 65, 86.

[87] Berle (11), 70–115, 180, and (18), 444, 445; Chandler (2), 314, 322; Drucker (3), 35, 99, 102, 340, 342; Einaudi, 282–83; Fortune, 99; Hoover, 275, 276; Maurer, 186; Reagan, 122, 124, 125; Sutton et al., 57, 58, 65, 86, 87, 155, 163, 165, 359.

short-term maximizing of profit familiar in the old-fashioned competitive market. Rather, it accepted such gains as would not disrupt a market dominated by a handful of firms but would provide earnings sufficient to keep stockholders satisfied while furnishing the bulk of capital needed for the firm to grow or at least hold its relative position.[88]

The idea that top management had developed into the legitimating element in big corporations had two facts of practice in its favor. First, as of the 1960's management had apparently won its place as the typical controlling element. In 1929 the Berle and Means count located control in management in 44 per cent of the two hundred largest nonfinancial corporations; such management control was wielded over 58 per cent of the assets of these corporations. In 1963 Larner's count found management control in 84.5 per cent of such corporations; such management control was then wielded over 85 per cent of the assets of these corporations. Among the five hundred largest nonfinancial corporations of 1963, this tally found management in control of 75 per cent of the companies; such management control was exercised over 81 per cent of the assets of these companies.[89] The second circumstantial support for management as the legitimating element was the steady implicit bias to this effect in the law of corporate organization from 1890 into the 1960's. That bias favored broad discretion and generously protected autonomy for those who held central direction of large firms. There was no substantial move over this long span to change this alignment of values in state law. The vigorous growth of new federal regulation affecting corporate finance from the 1930's on imposed significant new responsibilities on the working style of those in control. But this growth did not challenge or disturb the control which had evolved as typical among large companies. In prevailing opinion the steady trends of business practice and corporation law seemed to attest a deep-rooted acquiescence—whether or not an informed positive

[88] Berle (15), 87, and (18), 449; Larner, 54, 57, 69, 72, 99, 100, 105, 106, 107; Maurer, 186; Rostow (2), 58–59, 68–69, 71; Sutton et al., 86, 174.

[89] Larner, 8, 9, 37, 38, 39.

consent—to self-perpetuating management as the normal prime factor in the internal governance of large corporations.[90]

Despite this apparent implied acceptance, there was an underlying instability to management's position as the legitimating element in modern big-corporation power. The situation was unstable because after twenty years or more of talk of corporate statesmanship the idea lacked specific substance, in fact and in law. In law the one defined expression of the concept was the spread of judge-made and statute law in the states authorizing expenditure of corporation funds for philanthropic purposes. This apart, the law added no definition of standards or rules to spell out for what purposes or by what means management might properly make decisions other than in the interests of shareholders. If the idea of a permissible, and even desirable, broader range of justifications of corporation action had merit, it was strange that it had found so little expression in law.[91] This want of formal content matched a want of specific matter and product from the idea of corporate statesmanship as it was expounded and demonstrated by management itself. The notion seemed to be that big-company management should play a legislative role, seeking a fair apportionment of benefits and burdens among all sectors of the community affected by the corporation's activity. But from these declarations emerged little or no helpful specifications of what the vague standards might mean in action. In contrast to this vagueness, critics of corporate statesmanship found objective meaning and convincing functional justification in the traditional idea that the prime criterion of corporate performance should be profit won in market. Moreover, for all its frailties, official legislative process worked subject to the pull and haul of various interest groups competing in the legislative arena. How corporate management would provide a comparable arena was left undefined, though there

[90] Berle (1), 28–40, (3), 1050, 1067; Berle and Means, 127, 247, 279, 287; de Capriles, 4, 13–14; Dodd (7), 34, 35, 43, 51, (8), 273–75, (10), 9, 13, and (19), 1008; Katz, 179–81; Rutledge, 338, 340.

[91] Baker and Cary, 359; Katz, 181. *Cf.* de Capriles, 2, 13–14; Eells (1), 26, 40, 92–94, 189, 190, 361; Hoover, 268; Manne (1), 414–16; Moore, 140, 141, 144, 145; Rostow (2), 57, 60–69, 71; Stryker, 191; Sutton et al., 58, 155, 177, 263, 359. But *cf.* Berle (18), 442–44.

was considerable implication that no competition of interests was necessary where the detached good will of managerial philosopher kings would put all relevant values in proper array.[92]

If internal checks and balances did not convincingly legitimate the power resident in big modern corporations, and the competitive market no longer policed them in classical style, the situation spelled increase of legal regulation. For there remained the underlying, traditional demand that power be legitimate in the sense that it be responsible or accountable. It was symbolic of the positive force of this demand that Congress should pass the Sherman Act in 1890, just as the main current in the states turned to removing regulatory features from corporation law. The trend of state law meant that we accepted a type of corporate structure which gave generous scope and substantial autonomy to central control as of high value for economic growth; we would accept utility as legitimating this instrument. But our growing confidence in organization as a major new asset was accompanied by fresh conflicts of interest and new concerns generated by particular power or particular effects produced by the large enterprises which the new corporate instrument helped into being.[93] Thus the twentieth century saw the development of new special areas of federal regulation of business behavior, which in effect responded to the social impact of large corporation power—the extension of preventive antitrust law (the Clayton Act), stronger regulation of transport and communications (with broader roles for the Interstate Commerce Commission and creation of new regulatory bodies for air travel and for telephone, radio, and television), stringent controls upon public utility holding companies, provision of legal support and protection of collective bargaining, some measure of consumer protection, and various tax rules with significant indirect if not direct impact on corporate business practices (for example, limiting undistributed earnings and affecting the direction and pace of

[92] Bowen, 141–42; Eells (1), 268, 372 and (2), 87, 119–20; Gordon, 304–12, 327, 340–43; Hurff, 120; Katz, 192; Sutton et al., 33, 34, 43, 57, 58, 65, 359. But *cf.* Berle (11), 180, and (14), 50, 52, 54.

[93] Berle (14), 111, 112; Dodd (10), 6–8; Hornstein (4), 1:288; Maurer, 284; Rutledge, 305–8.

spending by definitions of tax-deductible expenses and depreciation allowances). State economic regulation developed with less marked concentration on problems likely to be specially relevant to big corporation activity. But there were state examples —the expansion of public utility regulation, protection of dealer franchises, administrative scrutiny of the financial soundness of new securities issues, air and water pollution measures, and industrial safety and accident compensation laws.[94]

We should not overrationalize a course of policy growth which, like the uses of law generally in our history, typically responded to particular conflicts, fears, or felt needs with little over-all direction. Nevertheless, there was functional meaning to the major shift that occurred in enforcing the responsibility theme of legitimacy upon the large corporation. This shift abandoned the nineteenth-century approach, which embodied regulation of business practice in the law of corporate organization as a consideration for granting corporate status, removed most regulatory features from corporation law proper, and created specialized bodies of regulatory law outside of the law of corporate structure. For the most part these specialized regulations dealt, not with defining the corporation's form or powers, but with assessing results of its behavior which affected the general community or which involved interests outside the enterprise but closely dependent upon the objectives and methods by which it used its power. The nineteenth century built regulations of corporate business into the law of corporate organization, because in the context of the times this approach seemed adequate to the range of current problems. Limits on the firm's allowed purposes, size, and authority would help prevent it from subverting the competitive market, which lawmakers trusted to safeguard general community interest. Such limitations, along with some on financial structure and practices, would also protect investors and creditors; these were the only specialized interests which mustered sufficient weight to command much attention from

[94] *Cf.* Berle (3), 1049; Dodd (3), 1145, and Berle (4), 1365; Berle (14), 935–36, 946; Chayes, 31, 32, 35; Dewing, 2:817, 1078; Dodd (8), 283–84; Drucker (1), 80, 85, 97, 99, 265, 266, and (2), 9–10; Johnson and Krooss, 325–29, 348; Loss, 1:viii; Reagan, 145, 147–48, 149.

lawmakers, who, along with the rest of their society, were mainly concerned with overcoming capital scarcity. However, by the 1920's, if not earlier, the economy had moved into a much more complicated situation. Technology changed business in ways which meant that the market could no longer be trusted to be the pervasive, impersonal policeman it had once been, or had once seemed to be. The new size and reach of corporate enterprises meant that their behavior affected a broader range of interests than before. Insofar as the market continued to be an effective disciplinary force, it did so necessarily only within the range of interests which yielded to a market calculus. But the effects of late-twentieth-century-style business corporations ranged beyond interests for which the market could reckon. At the same time, those pressing most effectively on legislatures wanted a corporation law which gave wide scope to central control in big companies; prevailing opinion—accepting the general utility of organization as a major economic asset—acquiesced.

Out of these varied lines of development we had yet, as of 1970, to achieve explicit, comprehensive criteria of the legitimacy of power held by large business corporations. In action, however, we had struck an adjustment between the themes of utility and responsibility as legitimating factors. The principal job of corporation law was to satisfy the requirement of utility by authorizing corporate structures which would allow strong centralized control to realize the organizational potential of the corporate instrument. True, corporation law should also provide for enforcing the corporation's responsibility to its immediate economic function—to be a profitable enterprise in conventional market terms—and to this end should continue to recognize roles for the stockholder electorate and the stockholder gadfly. But in the second half of the twentieth century law and practice had developed to make this a subordinate aspect. There was little room to question in which direction corporation law had the greater practical impact; it successfully endowed central control, while it had only dubious effect in helping stockholders to effective roles, either collectively or separately. We now relied primarily upon legal regulations external to the corporation's own constitution to enforce its responsibility to its immediate economic functions and to its broader social relations. So long as dominant opinion continued to accept the large business corporation as a legitimate constituent element in social power, this division of function between corporation law and regulatory law bearing on corporations' behavior and impact rather than on their internal governance seemed likely to remain.

Chapter III

Institutional Contributions to Policy

THE first two of these essays examined the content of public policy concerning the business corporation as that policy grew through years of polemic and practical accomodation. The processes of policy making are likewise a dimension of legal history; indeed, they are always so, because legal history refers to those aspects of social experience which are specially shaped by the structure and procedures of legal agencies. Thus, it is relevant to seek further perspective on law's dealings with the business corporation by estimating the relative contributions of constitution makers, legislators, judges, administrators, and lawyers. In addition, to attempt some judgment of the influence of businessmen upon events is simply to acknowledge that the relative impact of official agencies cannot be measured save by some comparison with private action.

Rank in the legal order dictates beginning with constitutional law. As concerns formal constitution-making processes, there is not much to say. Until the middle and late nineteenth century, state constitution makers said little about corporations. In a handful of cases, they spelled out legislative authority to grant charters of incorporation.[1] But under most state constitutions this authority was embraced within the broad, simple grant of "legislative power." [2] Thus the scope of state legislative authority was left to be defined in the first instance by legislative practice. In the absence of explicit constitutional declaration to the contrary, state courts accepted the legislators' practical defini-

[1] Davis, 2:9, and 9, note 1 (Pennsylvania, 1776; Vermont, 1786, 1793.)

[2] Angell and Ames, 64; Cadman, 3, 84, 87, 111; Goebel, xxv; Stevens (1), 102.

tions of their power; more to the point, litigants accepted legislative chartering authority and by failure to press the issue on the courts reflected pervasive community acceptance of the legitimacy of legislative determinations as to how far the corporate device should be used.[3] In a pattern marked out between 1840 and 1880 policy makers wrote into state constitutions bans or limitations on granting corporate status by special statutory charter. Significantly, this action was coupled with explicit or clearly implied reconfirmation of legislative authority to determine general policy on the availability of incorporation.[4] Given the thousands of special statutory charters theretofore enacted in the states, such authorizations as were now written for enactment of general incorporation acts amounted simply to acknowledgments of a basic authority long firmly established by legislative practice as part of the "legislative power." [5]

The framers likewise included no reference to corporations in the federal Constitution. As fitted the novelty of their problems, some question was raised in the Federal Convention whether authority should be explicitly given the Congress to create corporations, apparently with an eye to situations in which state powers might not be adequate. The record of their discussions is slight and somewhat ambiguous. The net of it seems to be that the point was rejected as unnecessary; Congress might provide for incorporation where suited to national purposes under the broad heads of legislative authority given it.[6] Thus, within their respective contexts, legislative authority in the matter was treated in substance the same for the Congress as for the state legislatures. Another issue raised in the Federal Convention and in some state ratifying conventions, but not thereafter seriously pressed, went, not to the general authority of Congress over incorporation, but to the different issue of possible grants of trade

[3] Angell and Ames, 64; *cf. id.,* 68. See Cadman, 3, 5; Handlin, 139, 143, 151–52; Heath, 313, 314, 323; Primm, 32, 54.

[4] *E.g.,* N.Y. Const., 1846, art. VIII, sec. 1; Wis. Const., 1848, art. XI, sec. 1. *Cf.* Dodd (23), 448–49.

[5] *Cf.* New York Constitutional Convention, 1846, Debates, New York, 517, 518.

[6] Davis, 2:12–15; Warren (1), 699–702; *cf.* Davis, 2:10, 11–12, 38; Henderson, 25–27; and Livermore, 67, 136 (Articles of Confederation).

monopolies.[7] A substantial body of federal constitutional law later emerged concerning the business corporation, but this was the product of judicial development of protections and limitations, legitimated under broad language of the Constitution which made no specific reference to corporations. We cannot say that what the judges later did exceeded, let alone ran contrary to, ideas which would have been acceptable to the sophisticated lawyers among the framers.[8] There is no evidence, on the other hand, to show that most of what the judges later did should not be estimated as in substance the judges' production.

The corporate instrument was to develop as a major factor in our social organization. Yet it is not surprising that the written constitutions did not embody any basic judgments upon the corporation, except—by their silence—to leave to the everyday lawmaking agencies such problems as its use might present. Late-eighteenth- and early-nineteenth-century distrust was directed less at corporate organization than at special operating franchises which might be given such groups. The economic power which made the large business corporation a major institution of social order in the twentieth century was partly the product of law, but not in ways foreseen in the formative years of our written constitutions. Moreover, it would have departed from a central concept of our constitutional order to have written into our constitutions provisions about the organization and processes of other-than-legal institutions of social order. Our constitutional tradition saw law as a marginal force in society— of critical importance, yet legitimate because it was marginal. We looked to other institutions to determine most of the content of social life: to the family, the church, and the market, to general education, and to the growth of disciplines of scientific and technical knowledge. We took this approach so much for granted as not generally to require formal statement. True, the contract clause protected the security of private commitments of resources. We made explicit declaration of the idea of separation of church and state in the First Amendment. And later the

---

[7] Davis, 2:14; Henderson, 19–20; Livermore, 67.

[8] *Cf.* Hammond, 60; Henderson, 21–22, 34, 45, 48; Mitchell, 348, 351, 354.

judges developed the substantive meaning of due process of law as including protection of relative autonomy for private action against arbitrary intrusions of public power. However, the contract clause, the First Amendment, and the due process clause were limitations on government, not specifications for nongovernmental institutions. The same was true of the later specific bans on incorporation by special legislation, which left legislatures free to fix terms for incorporation under general statutes. To leave within the general discretion of legislative and judicial authority the resolution of such public policy issues as might develop around the business corporation fit not only our constitutional tradition but also the needs for social invention and flexible adaptation to experience, which were sharply felt in a society of rapid, broad, and deep change.

Among the three branches of government under our constitutions, the executive could claim the oldest English inheritance of authority to issue corporate charters. The Crown might charter without act of Parliament, though Parliament had successfully asserted its title to set limits upon additional grants of monopoly and other special privileges of action. In the Crown colonies royal governors had issued charters under their general commissions, and the power had sometimes been assumed also by the proprietor in proprietary colonies. But we treated executive prerogative as a concept incompatible with the constitutional governments created upon independence; such authority as had resided in royal prerogative and as was not deemed inconsistent with our institutions went to the legislative branch. The point as to corporations was evidently seen as so clear as to produce but one challenge. In 1779 the New Jersey legislature forced the governor to retreat from a claimed right to charter a religious congregation. No more was heard of inherent executive authority in the matter.[9] Governors occasionally wielded the veto to enforce the later state constitutional bans on special charters, but this was a limited role.[10] Given the character of the new

[9] Cadman, 3–5; Dodd (23), 196; *cf.* Hurst (1), 397; Stevens (1), 102.

[10] Hurst (4), 411, 416; Kuehnl, 160–64; *cf.* Cadman, 128–31, 138–39, 159–60.

federal government as one of limited, delegated authority, it was even more plain that the President drew no title from precedents of Crown prerogative. President Jackson, of course, used his veto against the recharter of the Second Bank of the United States, but the grounds for this action were primarily objections to the special-action franchises of the bank and did not go to issues of coi porate being as such.[11] Federal executive power did not figure in public policy toward the corporation until the mid-1930's. Then, in legislation regulating the issue and sale of securities, Congress delegated authority to administrators, which was used in effect to put new content into some aspects of corporation law, relative in particular to management-investor relations.[12] In view of the late-eighteenth- and the steady nineteenth-century trend which made the legislature the agency to legitimate general policy, it was logical that executive authority drop out of the picture. We paid a price for this institutional logic—and not only in the field of policy concerning corporations. One practical result was that we lost what might often have been helpful executive leadership in giving living content to policy. Indeed, it was the realization of this cost—and the judgment that it was not acceptable—which brought the executive back into the policy-making arena in the mid-twentieth century through federal administrative regulation of corporate securities.[13]

Judicial power was not treated as including authority to confer corporate status on individuals by court decree. Incorporation created forms of social organization capable of action binding upon, or fixing rights of, third parties. Such action too closely touched the over-all allocation of power in society to be allowed out of the hands of the legal agency accepted as wielding the highest authority. At one time the Crown, this agency became in our English inheritance the legislature. Especially in the American setting, legislative authority won highest legitimacy because it rested in a numerous, popularly elected assem-

[11] Govan, 201–2; Hammond, 405–10; Hurst (1), 397.

[12] Dean, 698–706; Dodd (12), 930–46; Loss, 1:107–28, 2:866–68, 911, 1027–36.

[13] Dodd (14), 174, and (18), 255.

bly drawn from all corners of the polity. The traditional scope of the "judicial power" which our constitutions vested in courts stood in sharply limited contrast to the extent of law making once known in the Crown and later bestowed upon the legislature. Courts in our system built law in coral-reef fashion, piece by piece; they were not conceded authority to enact forms of social organization. Courts sat to dispose of focused controversies which suitors brought to them; they did not sit to issue licenses or otherwise legitimate frameworks for action. Courts worked under the tradition of evenhanded application of general law; they had no recognized function of apportioning privileges, of giving some men legal capacities not enjoyed by others. The generalization of legally recognized social forms, the legitimating of organizational patterns, the allocation of special legal capacities were all the business of legislatures.[14] Common law bulwarked the legislative monopoly by denying incidents of corporate status to private actors who held no statutory charter. However, it does not appear that the common law went so far as to treat unauthorized claims or pretensions to corporate status as a crime.[15]

The course of legal development put two qualifications upon the proposition that judicial power did not include authority to confer corporate status. One of these qualifications was more apparent than real. In some circumstances, where a just regard to reasonable expectations was taken to require such action, the courts would treat as a *de facto* corporation individuals who had claimed corporate status without proper warrant. But such judicial decision simply made equitable adjustments of particular relationships, especially to protect third parties. Rules about *de facto* corporate status operated only after the event, to resolve some disorder of relations and not to create a sanctioned pattern for future relations.[16] A more substantial type of qualification upon the want of common law capacity to create corporate status centered upon the readiness of the common law to

[14] *Cf.* Dodd (8), 262, 263, and (23), 21, 195–98; Freund, 39–42; Stevens (1), 104, note 10.

[15] Cooke, 99, 100, and 100, note 1.

[16] Stevens (1), 168, 169.

recognize broad presumptive powers of private contractors to shape agreements enforceable or recognized by law. As among the contracting parties, men might create judicially recognized relations similar to some of those which might also exist within the discipline of corporate organization; by contract, some men might confer agency powers on others, might bind themselves to abide by decisions of their delegates, and—as among themselves —might limit their respective liabilities for debts arising out of their common ventures. It did not require statutory sanction to create important kinds of authority and subordination within a group agreeing to act for common ends and by coordinated action. The scope which contract law gave individuals to contrive on their own initiative some counterparts of corporate organization was, however, a qualification of, rather than an exception to, the proposition that the common law might not create corporate status. Private contracts might not bind nonconsenting third parties in the way in which statutory incorporation might free stockholders from liability for corporate debts. Moreover, statutory incorporation provided a means of legitimating standardized patterns of dealing inside and outside an organized group with a firmness of outline and content which could be achieved only more slowly and at the price of greater uncertainty and variation through the growth of contractual customs. Want of quick and firm standardization of group discipline and third party relationships threatened such security of expectations as would best promote investment and venture; private contracting might, for example, by continuing *ad hoc* effort manage an indefinite succession of parties to a venture, but this could be done with more economy and certainty within forms of succession formally blessed by the legislature. Measured by men's behavior, the line was less sharp between incorporation under statute and group arrangements by private contract than formal doctrine might suggest; the content, if not the form, of incorporation under statute was largely the product of private will and push. Nonetheless, legislation legitimated, made binding, and standardized certain forms and contents of relationships beyond what purely private agreement could accomplish.[17]

[17] Dodd (2), 984, 985, 996, 1010; Hurst (2), 12, 15, 17.

A review of the roles of the major legal agencies after 1776 thus brings us to the legislature as the regular source of incorporation. The legislature's title would have been clouded had it depended on the colonial experience. In the colonial years incorporation derived largely from the Crown or from the Crown's delegates. But even colonial legislative bodies participated in granting charters.[18] In any event, the prime relevance of the colonial experience to later years is that whatever cloud it cast on the legislature's title threw into sharp relief the sweep of authority conferred in this, as in all other, public policy making by the unqualified grants of "legislative power" in the state constitutions. From 1776 through the 1820's state legislatures enacted several hundred special corporate charters for business enterprises, with a considerable diversity of content.[19] Legislative practice thus interpreted the constitutions so as to lay full claim to the policy-making discretion which the breadth of the constitutional language allowed.

This practical construction went for two generations without substantial challenge in the courts or from the executive or from general opinion.[20] Controversy flared into occasional political drama, as in the Pennsylvania contest over extending the life of the Bank of North America in 1785–87. Then, in the 1830's the question of rechartering the Second Bank of the United States provided a rallying point for a confused battle of interests and words.[21] Out of this combat came emotion-charged attacks on the legitimacy of statutory charters.[22] But there is a striking contrast between the high feeling surrounding such spotlighted episodes of controversy and the matter-of-fact style in which state legislatures continued throughout to produce special charters by the score. The contrast should counsel caution in interpreting what was afoot. If more weight is given to what was done than to what was said—and to do so seems appropriate,

[18] Davis, 1:16, 17, 18, 20, 25.

[19] Evans, ch. 3.

[20] Angell and Ames, 64, 68; *cf.* Bank of Augusta v. Earle, 13 Peters 519, 587 (U.S. 1839).

[21] Davis, 2:310–13; Hammond, 53, 369–404; Hartz (1), 236; Livermore, 259.

[22] Gouge, ch. IX.

given the sizable volume of chartering—there was never any serious challenge to basic legislative authority to determine the uses of the corporate device. Partisan debate sometimes ranged widely. But the heart of the matter was always a dispute over the terms on which incorporation might be available or over the grant of special franchises (notably the right to issue bank notes) apart from the grant of corporate existence. The first of these essays explored controversies over the wisdom of, as distinguished from the root authority for, legislative creation of corporations. The relevant point here is that these controversies never presented a substantial or continuing attack upon the validity of the legislature's claim to be full arbiter of the matter. The Jacksonian outcry against corporations, insofar as it was not in the main an outcry against banks and paper money issued by banks, proved in the end simply a demand that all should have reasonably equal access to the benefits of incorporation. Symbolic was the resolution of the matter in the New York constitutional convention of 1846: special charters were forbidden, save in cases for which the legislature could not adequately provide by general incorporation acts.[23]

From mid-nineteenth century on, state legislatures multiplied general incorporation acts to match the emerging pattern of constitutional bans on special chartering. By common acceptance this trend of policy was taken as continuing within a freshly defined framework a kind of legislative authority that had existed from the first years of independence.[24] Beginning with pathbreaking New Jersey legislation toward the end of the nineteenth century, state legislatures added a new and important item of practical construction in developing their constitutional authority to set terms of use for the corporation. The statutes now expansively endowed businessmen with authority to vary by charter or bylaws the terms which the law otherwise appointed for corporate organization and powers. By such practical interpretation, legislatures read their constitutional authority

[23] N.Y. Const., 1846, art. VIII, sec. 1. *Cf.* Angell and Ames, 57; Dodd (7), 28; Evans 11, table 5.

[24] Cooke, 93, 94; Dodd (23), 197, 198, 311, 312, 317; Hornstein (4), 1:65.

as including power to delegate to private agreement the definition of an increasingly important part of the content of business corporation charters. This meant that legislatures asserted authority to return the contrivance of business organization mainly to the realm of contract. Consistent with the past, this new turn in the definition of legislative authority went largely without direct challenge in court.[25] There was unease over the extending of such delegation of public policy making to private hands. But the tradition of sweeping legislative authority in this realm was strong. Hence this new unease found indirect expression. Some state courts in effect curtailed the operation of the statutory delegation by imposing what amounted to equitable limitations on corporation insiders or managers, as they wielded the powers which they had framed for themselves under what appeared to be the unqualified blessing of the statutes. Of similar practical impact was a growing body of federal law, partly through rules and decisions of the SEC and partly through federal court rulings under the federal securities legislation or the SEC's elaboration of that legislation.[26] The limitations on corporate management indicated by this new body of law made by judges and by federal administrators were significant. Likewise, however, the fact that these limitations were developed by indirection attested to the strength of the concept, built on some 175 years of legislative practice, of the legislature's formally complete power to define the terms on which men might organize corporations.

The development of judge-made and administrative law qualifying the formal sweep of statute-given corporate power reminds us that there is more to the history of legal process than the growth of separation-of-powers doctrine. Differences in formal organization and procedure among the major legal agencies have had operational reality. But these differences have been of a large generality. Hence they have gained working meaning only through specific content added by patterned trends in the

[25] Berle and Means, 127, 130–31, 247, 279, 287; Dodd (7), 35, 58, and (19), 1006–08; Hornstein (4), 1:64, 67; Stevens (1), 104, note 10.

[26] Berle (3), 1074; Dodd (10), 9, 12, 13, 37–46, (15), 139, 140, (19), 1007, 1008, and (23), 70–71; Gower (2), 1383, 1384; Hornstein (4), 1:527, 530, 541; Katz, 180, 184.

behavior of these legal agencies. Agency behavior has shaped, and been shaped by, agency structure and process. A useful perspective on public policy toward the corporation may be gained by asking whether legislatures, courts, and executive or administrative officers appear to have made different contributions to the whole body of law about corporations. It appears that they have and that these different contributions probably derive chiefly from the different organizational characters of the major legal agencies. Institutional inertia and institutional vested interests help fashion character, along with differences in the functional ends and capacities of agencies. There has been little of the detailed research needed to flesh out these propositions. But enough appears in the history of corporation law to suggest some main themes. Let us consider the relative contributions of statute law and judge-made law to the emergence of the corporation, the working significance of the era of special statutory charters, and the relative roles of state and federal lawmakers. Moreover, we must have in mind that for realism we need to weigh roles of legal agencies relative to the spheres of initiative of will and decision occupied by private actors.

From the first years in which we made much use of the corporate device, statute law defined the organizational framework and the basic terms on which the legal order would legitimate use of the corporation. The manner of creating corporations, the types of internal organization permitted, their allowed span of life, the limits of their capitalization, the range of permitted ownership or lender interests in them, and the procedures for making and amending bylaws and charters were matters in the first instance of statute law. This was the pattern well established in the span from about 1780 to 1840, which saw the broadening use and practical acceptance of the corporate instrument in business.[27] When major issues concerning the general terms of corporate organization arose in later years, they, too, found primary resolution in statute law. In the late nineteenth century statutes sanctioned holding companies.[28] When the pe-

[27] Dodd (7), 27, 29, (16), 812, and (23), 268, 269. *Cf.* Stimson, 2:ch.1.

[28] Brandeis (1), 556; Chandler (2), 30, 31; Dodd (7), 27, 30, 42, and (8), 274, 275; Hornstein (4), 1:26, 125.

riod 1920–40 brought bolder demands from promoters and managers for large leeway to write corporate articles and bylaws to extend their control, the movement obtained its legitimization through statutory revision.[29] There was underlying consistency in these matters over which legislation was the prime embodiment of law; all of them—even the enlarged delegation of power to private contrivance under the laws of the 1920's and 1930's—dealt with the basic terms of legal existence for corporations. This was legislative, not judicial, business. It was so for reasons of constitutional force; only to the popularly elected assemblies did we concede authority to deal with the social balance of power—which private group organization was bound to affect in the large—and to exercise the range of choice involved in defining such public policy as at one and the same time made broad generalizations (for example, that corporate organization was socially acceptable) and gave these generalizations particularly defined bounds and content (for example, that corporate organization was socially acceptable within specified limits and within specified styles of structure and procedure). Our tradition denied such scope of policy making to judicial power as a matter of constitutional law. In addition, inherent limitations in lawmaking by litigation made courts inappropriate agencies to create the general forms of corporations. Judges must find their policy-making opportunities wholly within the particular circumstances of the particular suitors and particular disputes brought to them, and this focus tends to emphasize the adjustment of the immediate situation of the parties rather than the structuring of relations among whole classes of individuals.[30]

Nonetheless, as one might expect, given the general sweep of common law growth in the nineteenth-century United States, judges made a great deal of the corporation law. True, judicial lawmaking in this field developed later than statute lawmaking. There were institutional reasons for this lag. Since incorporation required some kind of legislative sanction, statutes had first to legitimate corporations before there could be lawsuits over corporate affairs. Lawsuits, moreover, arise out of serious break-

[29] Dodd (7), 43, 44, and (19), 1006, 1008; Hornstein (4), 1:64, 66, 67, 69, 70, 71, 72, 80, 81.
[30] *Cf.* Stevens (1), 136, 137.

downs in relations—that is, usually out of abnormality. There had first to be a considerable, widespread use of the business corporation before any considerable number of lawsuits could arise to offer courts opportunities to contribute to corporation law. Further, the earlier years of use of the corporation were years in which there was rather scant reporting of judicial decisions in this country. Thus, corporation law grew almost entirely through the enactment of statutes from 1780 to 1830. The first edition, in 1832, of the first specialized treatise in the United States on corporations showed many doctrinal gaps and small beginnings and perforce drew substantially on English decisions, most of which did not deal with affairs of business companies. However, after 1830 judge-made law concerning business corporations grew fast and in volume.

State courts made much of this law, with little reference to the terms of the particular legislation under which corporate litigants existed; within the general legitimating framework of special and general incorporation statutes there tended to develop a kind of common law of corporations, representing a substantial amount of shared policy among the states' judicial lawmakers. In the dynamics of this growth it is true that the statutes played a part. It was functional in the hurried push of development in the United States that lawyers, lobbyists, and legislatures should economize by imitating each other. This tendency was promoted as corporations did more and more business across state lines and hence carried the models of their statutory organization outside the chartering state. Courts could build a considerable shared judge-made law of corporations because among the states both general and special corporation statutes showed sufficient similarity for judges of one state to feel relatively free in conscience to borrow from the judicial determinations of sister states. The force of circumstances combined with traditions of the judicial job to encourage courts to borrow from one another. There was typically too little litigation over corporate affairs in any one state to give its judges opportunity to develop a comprehensive body of corporation law out of their own decisions. By analogy to the inheritance of English common law, judges in the United States readily conceived of all doctrine applied in court as deriving from principles shared among sovereigns of like culture. Regard for judicial precedent reinforced courts' inclination to legitimate their rulings by fashioning a coherent pattern of policy out of scattered decisions. Courts sat more often and more continuously than legislatures, and it took only the resources of the suitors to shape an issue of which the judges must dispose; once the legislature had regularized the general frame of reference by providing incorporation, the courts by the nature of their organization and function were put under a greater variety and flow of demand than the legislature was to add content to the law concerning corporate behavior. We must not exaggerate the consistency of the judge-made law of corporations. There was in fact considerable diversity in it, natural to the extent and diversity of the country and the varying availability of legal source materials and the varying abilities, strategies, and philosophies of lawyers and judges. Conversely, we must not exaggerate the amount of difference among the state statute books. The matter defies close inventory. But over the span from 1780 to 1970 there emerged perhaps more predictable uniformity in the statute law than in the judge-made law of the business corporation in the United States.[31]

Judge-made law contributed a good deal of specific content to the organizational character of the corporation, as in defining the normal authority of corporate officers, the particular catalog of corporate powers, and the relative claims in law of different classes of investors and creditors. Thus, although the definition of legitimate corporate organization was basically the prime prerogative of the legislature, in practice the judges did a good deal to translate into particular operational terms the meaning of the corporate life bestowed by statute. If we look for some underlying division of labor between legislative and judicial policy making affecting the use of the business corporation, we shall not find it in any distinction which would rigidly confine the statutes to corporate organization and judicial decisions to matters other than corporate structure.[32]

Nonetheless, the sum of things suggests that differences in the

[31] Berle (12), 336; Berle and Means, 221; Dodd (8), 254, 256, 257, 262, 263, 279, 281, (10), 13, and (23), 6.
[32] Berle (7), 249, 250; Dodd (7), 27, (8), 282, 283, (19), 1008, (22), 526, 527, and (23), 2, 3, 268; Jennings (1), 193, 196, 197; Loss, 1:vii.

constitutional authority and the working character of legislative and judicial agencies led them to have principal effect upon different aspects of corporate operations. The legitimation of the corporation—the whole-package definition of the terms of its existence and of its structure and procedures—in the long run has been embodied in legislation. Of course legislatures lacked experience. Moreover, the pace and variety of our growth and the chronic nineteenth-century scarcity of means fostered crude and impatient improvisation among businessmen and lawyers. Thus, legislation left organizational gaps which judge-made law filled in from time to time; so it was, for example, with definition of the authority of corporation officers.[33] But when businessmen and their lawyers sought basic new directions in corporate organization, they turned back to the legislature. They did so to legitimate the holding company in the late nineteenth century. They did so in the 1920's and 1930's when they wanted to legitimate creation of articles and bylaws which would allow promoters or management to enlarge their control and maneuvering room vis-à-vis investors or bondholders. Likewise, when events provoked active concern that defects in corporate power structure harmed investor interests and the general economic and social interest in mustering capital and using it responsibly without fraud or waste, we resorted ultimately to legislation to establish new policy frames of reference. True, there was some growth in judge-made law against stock market manipulation, and from the last quarter of the nineteenth century until the 1930's litigation improvised procedures and doctrines to sanction reorganization of financially distressed corporations.[34] But by mid-twentieth century the center of policy in these matters was in the statute books—in state blue-sky laws and in federal legislation on bankruptcy and reorganization and securities issues and dealings. The more narrowly focused interests—those seeking a free field for promotion and management—wanted the legitimacy which only the legislature might confer; those

[33] Angell and Ames, 38, 95, 352, 597, 613; Berle (1), 46, 50; Berle and Means, 221; Byrne, 82–84; Dewing, 2:1288–89; Dodd (10), 13; Finletter, 1, 3, 8, 19; Hornstein (4), 1:63, 80, 81, 188, 189, 190.

[34] Stevens (1), 767, 772, 774, 776, 781.

concerned with the broader reach of the corporation into the operation of the economy wanted the fresh generalization of policy which only legislation could achieve.[35]

We can see the ultimate primacy of statute law over judge-made law in matters of corporate structure reflected in another aspect of the growth of policy. From time to time legislation established new structural concepts which at a stroke rendered considerable areas of judge-made law obsolete or of quite limited operational importance. By giving promoters and management practical freedom to obtain articles and bylaws enlarging their discretionary authority, statutes of the 1920's and 1930's far reduced the importance of a complex body of judge-made law concerning *ultra vires* action of corporations. Statutory validation of no-par shares rendered irrelevant substantial judicial learning on watered stock. By statute, management or controlling interests obtained such broad discretion to fix financial structure as to avoid preemptive claims, which judicial decisions had awarded stockholders. The Uniform Stock Transfer Act supplanted a good deal of complex court-made law on securities titles. Corporate reorganization sections added to federal bankruptcy law set new points of departure for matters which for two generations had been governed by judges' ideas of policy. Thus, if courts and legislatures from time to time shared policy-making leadership, where issues could be resolved by arrangements of corporate organization, statute law tended to dominate over the longer span. It was a dominance derived both from constitutional concepts of legislative power and from the differential utilities of legislative and judicial law-making processes.[36]

Law made by statute consistently yielded place to law made through adjudication (whether by courts or, later, also by administrators under broad statutory standards) in two somewhat analogous situations. One of these existed where the behavior of businessmen created reasonable expectations in other persons which the law should not in fairness allow to be defeated by the self-interest of those who generated the expectations. Out of

[35] Berle (6), 393; Dewing, 2:1288–89; Finletter, 1, 2, 8, 19.
[36] Berle (7), 250; Dodd (4), 785, (8), 282, 283, and (19), 1008; Hornstein (4), 1:188–90; Loss, 1:vii.

such appraisals courts developed much of their doctrine concerning the authority of corporation officers and agents when outsiders sought to hold the corporation to commitments made in its name. Of similar estoppel-like character was the doctrine of *de facto* corporations: to prevent or repair unjust damage to third parties, individuals who claimed corporate status must submit to having particular transactions treated in law as if done by a corporation, though by legal defect they lacked general corporate capacity.[37] Legal protection thus afforded to outsiders had its counterpart in doctrine protecting investors within the corporate circle who stood in vulnerable dependence upon the superior knowledge and capacities for decision of management or concentrated controlling interests. Out of particular contexts of dependence, judges—and, later, administrators empowered by federal statutes regulating corporate securities issues and trading—imposed some measure of fiduciary obligations on corporate insiders. The general law of trusts had been judge-made in the United States. Courts found themselves in familiar territory when they set standards of good-faith dealing for men who controlled assets in which the beneficial interests lay in other individuals. It was no barrier that the controlling men appeared to enjoy full discretion under the broad language of the corporation acts or of the corporate articles which the statutes legitimated; trust duties had long been laid by courts upon men who held formally absolute titles to property. However, the trust analogies did not mean that judges and administrators did not wield substantial new policy-making discretion as they held corporate insiders to account. They pressed past the more obvious imposition of fiduciary obligations on corporate officers and agents to recognize situations in which a controlling stock interest might lay its holders under like duties to fellow investors not in the inner circle. Moreover, they enlarged the concept of the kind of transactions which might be subject to measures of

[37] Baker and Cary, 352–58; Berle (7), 250; Dewing, 1:104; Dodd (8), 281, 282, 292, and (16), 815–17; Fleischer, 1150, 1151, 1152; Hornstein (4), 1:109, 401, 527, and 2:29, 32, 33; Manning (3), 252; Rostow (2), 51; Stevens (1), 620; Timberg, 558, 559. *Cf.* Berle (10), 935, and (16), 10.

good-faith rather than arm's-length dealing; the insider must not seek his own profit at the expense of the corporation's general assets or earning opportunities, but likewise he must not overreach his less knowledgeable fellow investors in their dealings in their shares.[38]

Thus, law made by adjudication was most distinctively law that qualified the use of corporate organization and powers by imposing equitable limitations on apparently unlimited authority. Law of this kind was more efficiently made by adjudication than by legislation. Such decisions were validated by appeal to standards of fair play and good faith, which might be grounded in legislation. But these standards were too general to affect life unless they were translated to obligations relevant to the specific circumstances or relations of individuals. Legislation could give impetus to this process, as did the federal statutes of the 1930's which made fresh declaration of principles of fair dealing between corporate management and investors and bondholders. Significantly, however, the innovative effects of the new federal acts dealing with corporate finance and reorganization emerged less from what Congress declared as substantive law than from the warrant which Congress gave the courts and federal administrators to build new case law. The utility of law declared in standards (for example, in requirements of good faith) rather than in rules (for example, in unqualified liability of directors for dividends impairing solvency) lay in its flexibility and continuing rationality in meeting the infinite variety and change of a market-oriented economy. Common-law-style policy making worked best in developing the content of standards and could obtain results of which legislative generalization was incapable. Case-by-case growth of law allowed experiment and limited commitment and the accretion of experience. The process was subject to the rational and emotional discipline of measuring decisions against the concrete competition of focused interests of identified individuals who would be helped or hurt in quite specific ways by what the tribunal decided. We must reckon, too, with the realities of mustering the initiative and energy of will

[38] Baker and Cary, 52; Dodd (8), 281–82, 293; Hornstein (4), 1:27; Stevens (1), 139, 140, 169, 771–76.

and the inducements needed to persuade public officers to make law. Legislative machinery was better geared to adopting or rejecting policy proposals brought to form and given impetus from outside the legislature than to initiating policy through the cumbersome operations of a numerous assembly, sensitive to diverse constituencies and meeting only at intervals and for limited times. The demand of a single claimant or a few claimants could put in motion regularly sitting courts or administrative tribunals; no large coalition of supporting interests need be mobilized; unhampered by general indifference and insulated from the pressures of narrow constituencies, courts and administrative tribunals had freedom to exercise creativity upon issues too particular to command the attention of legislatures. Of course, adjudicatory lawmaking fell short of ideal fulfillment: litigants might present too narrow a focus to show the full relevant range of social interests involved; lawyers might not be of comparable competence to assure adequate help to the tribunal from all quarters of the controversy; the decision makers might lack insight for the relevant issue or skill to use the facts of the immediate case to escape bad precedent by distinguishing it and to point growth in a promising direction. Even so, the standards aspects of corporation law—as distinguished from legal provision of corporate title and the frame and machinery of corporate organization—derived their substance and their dynamics so clearly from adjudicatory processes as to indicate that basic functional reasons assigned the lead role here to judges and to administrators acting like judges.[39]

Between the distinctive roles of legislation (in fixing forms of corporate organization and validating standards of corporate behavior) and of law made by adjudication (in developing the specific equitable content of standards of fair play and respect for reasonable expectations), we must insert the twentieth-century role of preventive administrative action, most notably through the SEC. With authority to generalize out of its experience of specialized concern with corporate finance—and power

[39] Berle (1), 46, 50; Berle and Means, 221; Dodd (10), 13, 37–46, and (19), 1007; Hornstein (4), 1:63, 80, 81, 527, 530, 541; Katz, 179; Loss, 1:vii.

to aid generalization with particular rules open to more flexible revision and amendment than could usually be accomplished in statute law—the SEC represented a new potential in public policy making. In promise, at least, there lay in this kind of agency qualitative differences of law-making capacity, which put the legislation establishing it in a wholly new category from statutes which had their impact either by direct legitimation of forms of corporate organization or through the slow, often episodic and chance incidence of subsequent litigation. The SEC made its preventive contribution to a more healthy condition of corporate behavior chiefly through its power to set the terms for registering new securities issues and for soliciting stockholders' proxies. Effective by warning and guideline, such preventive action operated through the SEC's rule-making, rather than its adjudicative powers. Because the SEC had such preventive impact through its legislative type of activity in some areas of corporate behavior, it is the more striking that it made itself felt in other areas by law made through adjudication. It was by case-by-case accretion of decisions that the SEC and federal courts interpreting the SEC statutes and SEC rules thereunder employed the new federal statutory framework to add content to standards for good-faith behavior of management toward investors.[40] This record reminds us that differences between legislative and adjudicative styles of lawmaking are not merely formal but serve to produce different kinds of policy.

After comparison of statutory and adjudicatory contributions, the most striking institutional aspect of the growth of corporation law was the flow of special acts of incorporation from about 1780 to 1875. For total volume and continuity over more than two generations, the production of such special charters stands out as one of the most conspicuous phases in the history of the legislative process in the United States—the more so in contrast to the practically total disappearance of such legislation from the last quarter of the nineteenth century on. We do not have a full inventory for all states. Totals varied among states, mainly according to differences in their economies. New Jersey saw a total of 2,318 special charters for business corporations

[40] *Cf.* Hurst (3), 47, 139–40, 153; Pound (1), 114, 137–38, 140.

from 1791 to 1875, when a constitutional provision barred further legislation of this kind. Even Wisconsin, in a less well-established economic environment, enacted 1,130 special charters for business corporations from 1848 until the practice was ended by a constitutional amendment effective in 1872. Through the greater part of the nineteenth century most state legislatures passed a considerable number of special charters, so that the country-wide sum ran into thousands.[41]

The first of these essays dealt with the substantive policy implications of this era of special charters. Here it is relevant to ask whether the flow of special charters gained any of its impetus and substance from legal institutional factors—from the nature of the nineteenth-century state legislature—and whether this flow in some ways may have influenced the working character of the legislative branch.

With no substantial exception, to 1800 and for some years beyond legislatures provided incorporation only by special charters; the business corporation had already become a familiar, if not yet a common, device before it was first dealt with by general legislation.[42] Special chartering continued to be the dominant style of legislative dealing with incorporation until the 1870's. At least from the New York manufacturing corporation act of 1811 and the 1837 Connecticut general incorporation act for business enterprises, legislative output overlapped special chartering with the creation of two kinds of general statute. One of these was the general incorporation act, which provided a single procedure to sanction the organizing initiatives of entrepreneurs. The other was a statute which defined certain incidents of corporate organization and powers which should apply to all corporations under special or general-act charter, barring special exemption. In addition, the pattern of legislative activity in this span from the 1790's into the 1870's included considerable amending of special charters—and sometimes also charters issued under general acts—usually to meet felt needs of busi-

[41] Baker and Cary, 937–39; Dodd (4), 785, (15), 140, and (17), 1258; Loss, 1:vii.

[42] Cadman, 205; Evans, 10, 11, 14–15, 17–18, 26–30; Kuehnl, 143.

nessmen to adapt their charters to their experience or to changing market exigencies.[43]

There is much in the working nature and the environing circumstances of state legislatures to suggest that special chartering
dominated the field for so long because of inadequacies of the
legislative process rather than for reasons of calculated policy.
Legislatures were slow to come to a principal focus upon enactment of policy generalizations; through the years of special corporate charters the session laws were also crowded with hosts of
private and local laws granting particular action franchises (to
build dams, for example), creating particular units of local
government (charters of cities and towns), establishing local
courts, and in earlier years granting particular divorces or sanctioning adoption of children in particular cases. Most nineteenth-century state legislatures were made up of men of limited
experience in public affairs, elected for short terms, and meeting
in short sessions; there was a considerable turnover of membership and a minimum staff. Coupled with the general impatience
of the times to get on with economic growth, these legislative
characteristics inclined legislators to deal closely with the immediate pressures for action put upon them, to imitate models
handiest for borrowing, to attempt little investigation or fact col-
lecting, and to invest little effort in trying to construct large
frames of policy. We see reflection of these operating habits in
the fact that private and local laws occupied from three to fif-
teen times the printed bulk of general laws, that legislative records in the states typically include no published findings based
on hearings and no published committee reports, and that only
in rare instances did a legislature provide the mechanism for
any between-sessions study of a generalized policy area with
preparation of recommendations for action. Symbolic of the
working atmosphere was the fact that until well into the nineteenth century legislatures operated by select committees—each
committee named *ad hoc* to deal with one bill—and that the
standing committee with jurisdiction over a broad, coherent sub-

[43] Dodd (7), 28, and (23), 3, 196, 197, 198 and 198, note 13; Evans
10. *Cf* Dodd (8), 264, and 264, note 52, and (23), 265.

ject-matter field became standard apparatus only after several decades had helped form more opportunistic and fragmented styles of approach to legislative problems.[44]

Such elements appear too plainly in the record not to be given weight in explaining the primacy of special chartering over general incorporation acts. Yet the institutional limitations of the legislature do not seem a sufficient explanation. These legislatures were not incapable of generalizing policy. General incorporation acts were early created for nonbusiness corporations: For religious congregations we find such general legislaion in New York in 1784, New Jersey in 1786, and Delaware in 1787. General acts provided incorporation for a broad range of charitable, religious, and literary purposes in Pennsylvania in 1791 and for libraries in New York in 1796 and in New Jersey in 1799. Fire companies might be chartered under general acts of Virginia of 1788 and of Kentucky of 1798.[45] With reference to incorporation for profit-seeking enterprise, New York in 1811, Connecticut in 1837, and more and more states in the 1840's and 1850's provided general incorporation laws for more-or-less-limited fields of business or enacted general provisions on corporate powers and limitations which applied to any corporation chartered in the given state under special or general act unless particular exception was made.[46] Such a record forbids us to think that it went beyond the talent or imagination of early nineteenth-century legislators to put all incorporation within generalized procedures and terms. Moreover, we must take care that we are not misled by the volume and seeming variety of the special charters. Close examination of the details of such charters will show the presence of a good deal of predictable regularity in form and content. The quantity of special charters was itself a factor which tended to breed imitation and unacknowledged standardization of terms. When the legislature

[44] Cadman, 15–17, 112, 114, 115, 116, 118, 121–22, 136, note 115, 153–54; Dodd (8), 263, 273 and 273, note 85, and (23), 198, 270, 361, 388, 417, 418; Heath, 312; Hornstein (4), 1:64, note 3, 65.

[45] Cadman, 9; Hurst (1), 51–52, 58–59; Pound (2), 39, 49, 53, 65, 67–68.

[46] Cadman, 5–7; Davis, 2:17, 234; Howe, 45–46.

dealt with some railroads or banks, there were likely to be true special circumstances or special impacts to be reckoned with. But the bulk of charters dealt with businesses which fell into classes in which any one firm was not in economic or social significance materially different from another firm in the field. In this situation, which embraced the great quantity of special charters, the volume of the chartering business brought to legislatures, coupled with the underlying likeness of the problems, rapidly built a common store of experience and encouraged matter-of-fact adoption of standard clauses.[47] Granted that it operated too much by rule of thumb and with a responsiveness to particular petitions which belonged more to courts than to legislatures, the nineteenth-century legislative branch accomplished more generalization of policy than is at first apparent. Its inadequacies in this respect do not offer a fully convincing explanation of its long-continued fondness for special chartering.

The more basic reasons for use of special charters thus appear to lie in the combination of public policy concerns and businessmen's desires explored in the first essay. In the early years special chartering reflected the habits of legal thought and the concern with the power of organized groups which found shorthand expression in the concession theory of the corporation: that the sovereign's act not only was necessary to create corporate status but also fully determined the content of that status. But as legislative practice eroded the reality of the concession theory, businessmen pressed effectively for special charters because they could thus be free of limitations on corporate behavior declared in the general statutes.[48]

Nevertheless, special corporate charters did disappear from the 1870's on, until by 1900 practically all incorporation was under general act.[49] Again, the substantive policy trends discussed in the first essay offer the core explanation for the disappearance of special charters. But the record indicates that con-

[47] Note 44, *supra.*

[48] Cadman, 69; Dodd (8), 263, 287, and (23), 198, 199, 244–45, 255; Hurst (4), 417.

[49] Cadman, 165–67, 169–70; Dodd (21), 1478, and (23), 386, 418; Hurst (4), 418–22; Kuehnl, 146–47.

cern with institutional factors—with the efficiency and integrity of the legislative branch as such—contributed to this outcome.

It is plausible that corruption was a substantial element in the enactment of special charters. The idea readily attaches to the very fact that special legislative action is taken—of obvious benefit to a few individuals thus singled out from the general community. The suspicion may be reinforced if variations appear in the texts of such charters. Also after optional general incorporation acts were available, businessmen continued to obtain special charters which omitted various restrictive provisions of the general acts. Such distrust was a component of the egalitarian feeling which impelled criticisms of corporate status and the movement at least to supplant special charters with incorporation under general laws.[50]

However, the record does not substantiate charges of large-scale corruption of the legislative process in enactment of special charters for business corporations. Legislative journals show that substantially all who sought incorporation obtained it; such a record offers little basis for finding that many bought a corporate status which others could not get. The bulk of special charters contained only provisions relevant to ordinary corporate operations. Most variations in charter texts were variations of operational arrangements conveying no implication of sinister ends against public interest. The amount of variation must not be exaggerated; over a relatively short span of years, special charter provisions tended to fall into standard patterns, as much as if they had been parts of general laws. This was true of the omissions in special charters of certain regulatory provisions contained in optional general incorporation acts; the omissions, too, fell into a pattern, so that they represented, not particular favors to particular incorporators, but a more lenient style of charter which businessmen as a whole could obtain from legislators.[51] Given the extent of standardization of special charter contents, the objective of corrupt approach to legislators

[50] Berle and Means, 136, 137; Evans, 11, 31; Hornstein (4), 1:65; *cf.* Dodd (23) 287, 288.

[51] *Cf.* Berle and Means, 137, note 15; Dodd (8), 263, 287; Hofstadter, 57.

—if there was corruption—must have been to obtain a special charter at all, rather than to obtain individualized favors in the corporate structure or corporate powers of any given company. To say this does not rule out the possibility of corrupt inducements. Legislatures sat only at intervals and for limited periods; there was enough of a press of business upon many legislative bodies for corrupt legislators to demand a price to prevent delay or for their own gain to expedite a given bill, to allow a particular application to win out in competition for limited legislative time and attention. Conceivably some such extortion was practiced.[52] But this kind of misbehavior spelled less danger to public welfare than generalizations about legislative corruption usually imply; it could not be widely employed without publicizing itself to destruction, and it did not seek positive privilege at public expense. Moreover, insofar as corruption sought special gain, the major incidents did not concern the grant of corporate status but the grant of other franchises enabling the grantees to engage in some action barred to the general public or to be free of legal burdens which would attach to the general public. The well-publicized episodes of bribery, logrolling, and conflict of interest involved grants of public land or money in aid of railroads, franchises to dam navigable streams, or to build navigation aids and exact tolls for their use, and the like. Of course, there was no less reason to value legislative integrity in these situations than in others. But these grants of action franchises bore on a narrower range of the economy than would have been involved by wholesale corruption in grants of corporate status for all business. Moreover, there was substantial legislative sifting of the terms both of proposed action franchises and of corporate franchises; few such bills passed as they were introduced, and much of the amending in course of passage limited the promoters' freedom to the advantage of third parties or the general community. In any event, there is the matter of relevance. Our attention in these essays focuses on the legislature's role in creating corporate status. Whatever dubious maneuvers went on in granting other kinds of franchise, there is little convincing evi-

[52] Cooke, 93; Dodd (7), 28, and (23), 314, 382; Hurst (4), 410–12, 416, 417. See notes 48, 49, *supra*.

dence that legislative integrity was seriously impaired in grants of the franchise to be a corporation.[53]

It is not enough, however, to conclude that handling the special charter business did not in fact materially hurt the integrity of legislative process. We in our time may thus realistically assess the past. But the nineteenth century did not necessarily see its situation as we see it. As the flow of special charters ran faster, some contemporary opinion feared its impact on legislative virtue. Thus in 1825 a New York legislative committee argued for a "free" (general-incorporation) banking law to prevent scandals in special chartering. In 1846 New York,—and subsequently others who followed its lead—sought to police special chartering by creating a constitutional presumption in favor of incorporation under general act; the new constitutional provision required the legislature to find reason why this procedure would not serve a particular need, as prerequisite to granting a charter by special statute. Fear of corruption and logrolling was expressed in a New Jersey governor's unsuccessful effort in 1855 to use the veto to halt special chartering, and like concern was voiced by New Jersey's governor in urging replacement of special charters by a chartering procedure under general laws in 1871.[54] However, like some later commentators, such contemporary expressions blurred the line between grants of corporate status and grants of other action franchises. And even taking at face value such nineteenth-century argument as we find along these lines, the sum of it does not add up to an impressive part of the movement to bring all incorporation under general legislation.

Ironically, in view of the moral fervor spent in attacks on corporate privilege, a more matter-of-fact consideration seems to have weighed heavier against special chartering. With increase in the volume of such statutes worry and irritation increased over the amount of scarce legislative time this business claimed. We hear this argument for general incorporation acts toward midcentury. It had become a point of prime emphasis by 1870. Thus, in Wisconsin the saving of legislative time was

[53] Hurst (4), 863, note 105.
[54] *Cf.* Robert S. Hunt, ch. 1; Hurst (4), 228, 257–58, 266–69.

the principal ground urged by the governor in supporting the proposal for a constitutional ban on special charters which the voters ratified to become effective in 1872. The relative speed with which such a constitutional limitation became standard among the states in the last quarter of the nineteenth century, suggests that the argument from overloaded legislative dockets appealed to a common experience with jamming of legislative business.[55] Certainly there was no widespread concern with legislative scandal to explain the trend.

We have been considering what effects on public policy toward the business corporation may have proceeded from the particular institutional character of the legislative, executive, and judicial branches. Realism enjoins that we add another institutional factor: federalism. The more important any legal theme is in United States history, the more likely it is that it has been significantly affected by the coexistence and interplay of the national and the state governments. The federal ingredient has not always been a product of deliberation. National and state legal agencies have generated their own institutional inertia and vested interests; the separate, yet interwoven, existence of nation and states has mandated or fostered situations and trends of action and result beyond what men perceived or planned or chose. But whether we see more of deliberation or of drift in any given area of public concern, we must still count the federal factor as a large part of much of the growth of public policy. It was so of law concerning the corporation.

The separate existence of the states as policy makers had the earlier and more marked effects upon law as it touched the business corporation. In contrast, the separate existence of the national government through the nineteenth and the early twentieth century had quite limited positive impact on use of the corporate device and was felt chiefly through particular limits put on state action.

That for a long time state law had a much more affirmative influence in this field than did federal law did not derive from inherent defect of federal authority. Experience was to prove that

[55] Cadman, 138, 156, 163; Dodd (7), 28, and (23), 287; Hammond, 572, 579; N.Y. Const., 1846, art. XI, sec. 1.

the federal Constitution—and especially the commerce clause —allowed Congress very broad authority to set the legal framework for business conducted through interstate channels and in national or sectionwide markets.[56] However, this was a potential endowment, the scope of which would be realized only through the interaction of national economic growth and the responsibilities and pressures which this growth would bring upon the national government. From 1790 to the 1930's the federal role was limited, not by formal bounds of the Constitution, but by a working tradition of the federal system. Though the Constitution was a charter potentially for a national government of broad capacities, it was the product of practical men, who were dealing with particular problems demanding strong central authority, and who were content for the time to meet their most immediately felt challenges. The Constitution also represented a political bargain, key terms of which assumed the continuing vitality of the states as prime lawmakers in most affairs; even on these terms the bargain had been concluded on too narrow a margin in the state ratifying conventions to encourage early assertion of the full possible range of federal authority. The Supreme Court never ruled that the Tenth Amendment prevented Congress from preempting the field of corporation law, for Congress never made so broad an assertion of power as to present the question. Before the Civil War, Congress chartered only two business corporations, and these—the First and the Second Bank of the United States—for highly specialized purposes. After 1860 Congress chartered transcontinental railroads and provided a general incorporation act for national banks. Again, the purposes focused on specialized national objectives. These instances of federal incorporation of business enterprises involved no attempt to set standards for the internal organization or external relations of business corporations in general; Congress's concern with the corporate device here was incidental to creating a politically more unified country and providing a more assured framework for the general growth of the national economy through a continental transport network and a national cur-

[56] Cadman, 11; Dodd (7), 28; Hartz (1) 42; Hurst (4), 416; Kuehnl, 58, 114, 165, 166; see note 50, *supra*. *Cf.* Dodd (23), 316.

rency. As Congress ventured into further use of its commerce power, it did so by regulations external to the structure of business organization—in the Interstate Commerce Act and in the Sherman Act and their successors. Throughout, to the 1930's, the practice of Congress assumed that legitimization of corporate structure and procedures and adjustment of the interests most immediately affected by corporate organization were the business of the states.

The strength of this traditional allocation of roles was attested by the fact that through the first half of the twentieth century recurrent proposals for exclusive federal incorporation of interstate businesses never mustered enough support to win serious consideration from Congress. Even in the years of New Deal crusading zeal, federal incorporation failed to move beyond the status of an interesting topic for speculative debate.[57] Moreover, when the Congress did act in the 1930's in matters of important effect upon corporate structure and practice, it did so, not by any general code, but piecemeal by regulating corporate security issues and proxies and by providing a new frame of reference for reorganization of financially distressed firms.[58] In its own specialized areas the federal intervention had bite and tended to build particular bodies of federal corporation law. This fact simply underlined the toughness of the tradition that Congress should not preempt the whole field. The contrast emerges, for example, through SEC rules which gave stockholders the right to have "proper" proposals put to corporate meetings. Recognizing that Congress did not wish to take over wholesale the definition of corporation law, the SEC declared that what was a "proper" subject should be determined by the law of the corporation's domicile. However, mid-twentieth-century general incorporation laws of the states typically allowed much of the internal structure and procedures of corporations

[57] McCloskey, 184–86; Stern (1), 645, 883, and (2), 823. *Cf.* Dodd (7), 930–46.

[58] On federal authority: Dodd (7), 51–59, and (23), 2, 7–8, 32–34, 38–41; Hornstein (4), 1:63; *cf.* Davis, 2:10, 11, 12, 15, 38; Livermore, 67. On federal incorporation: Dodd (12), 930, (16), 813, and (17), 1258; Rutledge 340.

to be set by the charter or bylaws, which were likely drawn to enlarge the prerogative and protections of management. The SEC hence took the position that it was bound by state law where state statutes or court decisions directly fixed the bounds of stockholder authority, but that SEC rules might supersede limits put by charter or bylaw upon stockholders' use of the proxy machinery. If the state took specific responsibility, its judgment would be followed; however, if it delegated broad control of the corporation's constitution to private decision, the concern of the federal policy for investor interests might not thus easily be put aside. Upheld by the courts in this distinction, the SEC tended to build its own law on the proper scope of stockholder use of the proxy machinery; given the indefiniteness of typical state statutory law in the matter, the SEC's decisional law tended to shape state law, rather than the other way round. But the vigor of federal law here was shown only in proportion as the states did not choose to make strong and definite use of what was clearly conceded to be their prerogative.[59]

Congress conceded to the states the primary role in making law legitimating the organization and procedures of business corporations. But the Supreme Court of the United States wielded its share of national power with more vigorous effect upon the use of the corporation. The *Dartmouth College* case put states on warning that regulation of their corporate creatures must be compatible with the contract clause of the federal Constitution. Concerned to respect state control of corporate activity, the Court took pains to deny that a corporation was a "citizen" of the chartering state so that it might claim in other states the benefits of the Constitution's privileges and immunities clause. But, at the same time, in *Bank of Augusta v. Earle* the Justices boldly erected a presumption of comity among the states under which a corporation might transact business under the protection of local law in states other than its domicile, unless a nondomiciliary state set specific barriers or limits upon the corporation's entry. From the end of the nineteenth century the Court developed doctrine that a state might not impose conditions on the entry of a foreign corporation which violated

[59] Dodd (18), 274; Fleischer, 1147, 1153, 1177; Stevens (1), 9.

commerce-clause protection of national markets, threatened corporate litigants' access to federal courts, or asserted extra-territorial jurisdiction or violated procedural fair play contrary to guarantees of the Fourteenth Amendment.[60] Conceptions of the legal character and the social uses and dangers of the corporation deeply colored the ideas of national interest which the Court pursued. Because so much of what the Court did turned on its evaluation of the social significance of the corporation, these developments have already been noted in the first of these essays. What is relevant at this point is another fact: It was the existence of the Supreme Court which provided the means to define and enforce values of the corporate style of business which could be realized only through law above and beyond the sovereignty of any one state.

The record prompts the question, why did Congress make only limited and piecemeal use of its potential power over corporations in interstate commerce, while the Court made national authority felt over a broad range of the states' involvement with corporate business. The contrast derived from the structure of national legal agencies rather than from different attitudes toward the corporation. The political environment in which we created our federalism inhibited early, bold use by Congress of its potential powers. The principal relevant judicial power conferred by the federal Constitution ran only to cases arising under the Constitution or laws of the United States. Under this head, the Court's creativity could be exercised only to sanction positive action by Congress (as in *McCulloch v. Maryland*) or to put limits upon the states (as by invalidating unconstitutional conditions which states attempted to lay upon entry of foreign corporations to do business). The only avenue which federal courts could take to contribute by their own force to positive law establishing corporation structure or powers was their further jurisdiction over controversies between citizens of different states. The Court established a formula which acknowledged state-chartered corporations as defendant-litigants in federal court, originally as an expression of distrust of corporate power

60 Loss, 2:900–909; *cf. id.,* 1:72, 73, 79, 80 (constitutional leeway for applying state blue-sky laws).

vis-à-vis that of individual complainants. But corporations which might be made defendants could also claim standing as plaintiffs under the diversity-of-citizenship jurisdiction. Thus the doctrinal inertia of federal law made federal courts an important forum for cases brought by, as well as against, business corporations. In *Swift v. Tyson* (1842) the United States Supreme Court asserted a vague authority in diversity-of-citizenship cases to make its independent determination of principles of general jurisprudence and commercial law. This claim did not run to supplanting state statute law, which an act of Congress always made the rule of decision in federal courts where applicable. Inescapably, however, confronting issues on which state law was unclear or silent, federal courts made some corporation law in diversity-jurisdiction cases and fashioned some rules contrary to those familiar in the judge-made law of corporations in the states. Such federal rules were notably important in defining the bases for shareholders' derivative suits and for equity receiverships of corporations in financial difficulty. But, no more than state courts could federal courts create corporations; the framework of corporation law continued to be built by state legislation. Generally, within this statutory frame, lawmaking by federal judges merged with lawmaking by state judges. The Court overruled *Swift v. Tyson* in 1938 to make state judge-made as well as statute-made law the rule of decision where applicable in suits in federal court. The change might be important for particular doctrines of corporation law. But, over-all, federal judges had not taken so leading a role in making corporation law as to make the change a major one.[61]

Thus we come back to the restrictive role of federal authority. Conceivably Congress might have undertaken to police the channels of interstate commerce against state encroachments. In *Gibbons v. Ogden* Marshall had outlined a broad power of Congress to issue licenses of free passage for business into multistate markets; Congress could wield such a licensing power to curb misuse of state law without purporting to take over the whole making of law for corporations. However, Congress made only limited and rather episodic use of its licensing power to

[61] Henderson, chs. III, IV, VII, VIII.

protect interstate use of the corporation.[62] To move Congress to action in any matter typically required mustering a broad range of interests. With its political roots in local constituencies, Congress was not readily brought to thwart local selfishness. Moreover, there were many states, and many lobbies were active in state legislatures on behalf of diverse interests; from these seedbeds challenges to national economic interest could grow in more variety and with more speed than the cumbersome machinery of federal statute making could easily match. The Court's processes were better adapted than those of Congress to curb state action burdening national interests. The Court need not placate local constituencies. It needed only the determination of a few litigants and the agreement of a handful of Justices to bring a matter in issue and to make some resolution of it. The Court sat in regular Terms which made it handily available. Litigation could be shaped to each particular new form of state challenge to national policy; at the same time, the Court must work within the limits of any given lawsuit, and hence, more appropriately than could Congress, the Court could narrow its work and thus insulate itself from the criticism and pressures which broad-sweep legislation was likely to arouse. Thus its structural character, both as court and as agency of superior national authority, encouraged the Supreme Court to a specially vigorous—because limited—role in determining the impress the federal system would have upon the sum of law affecting the business corporation.[63] This remained chiefly a role of surveillance against state parochialism until the 1930's when federal statutes affecting corporate securities created a new and unprecedented opportunity for federal administrators and federal judges to build an influential body of federal law on relations of management and security holders.[64]

[62] Ballentine, 358; Berle (7), 250; Bunn, 262, 266; Finletter, 25, 26; Henderson, ch. IV; Tunks, 284–87.

[63] Gibbons v. Ogden, 9 Wheaton 1 (U.S. 1824); Pensacola Telegraph Co. v. Western Union Telegraph Co., 96 U.S. 1 (1878). *Cf.* Hurst (2), 44, 48–50.

[64] On comparative legislative and judicial roles: Holmes, 102; Hurst (3), 139–40, 153. On Congress's expanded role from the 1930's: de Capriles, 12, 13; Dean, 698–706; Dodd (18), 274; Stevens (1), 9.

The separate existence of the states introduced a distinctively federal theme in the growth of corporation law through influences which first fostered diversity and then increasing uniformity among state corporation statutes. Diversity was an unplanned, though functionally natural, beginning for this history; the trend toward uniformity began, paradoxically, out of planned diversity, which induced more and more planned conformity.

From 1790 through most of the nineteenth century circumstances encouraged the separate existence of the states to foster variations in the development of corporation law. Men in a hurry were inclined to imitate when they could find models; from the 1820's on there was obvious borrowing of statutory provisions among legislative draftsmen. On the other hand, state legislatures of the early nineteenth century were crudely equipped for their jobs; though imitation fostered a trend toward uniformity, for want of much knowledge of what was going on elsewhere, most development in any given state's legislation built on what had gone on within its own borders. Because sufficient decisions were wanting in most jurisdictions to supply a comprehensive body of judge-made law, and because courts habituated to making common law easily adapted the analogy of that process to fill in the detailed content of statutory corporation law, there was more overt interstate borrowing by courts than by legislatures. However, lacking any single authoritative voice, the state courts diverged in policy in important respects, as in the relative strictness or leniency with which they dealt with *ultra vires* action of corporations, with the gains of promoters, and with charges of watered stock.[65] Growing experience with the use of the corporation tended to standardize businessmen's conceptions of the kind of corporate instrument they wanted. Thus special charters and then the general incorporation acts of the later nineteenth century began to show increasing uniformity of pattern. When changed demands from

[65] *E.g.,* Angell and Ames, 532 ff.; de Capriles, 5, 6; Dodd (8) 256, 257, and (10), 15; Hornstein (4), 2:26, and (3), 441, 443–45; O'Neal, 1:161, 162, 191, 207; Stevens (1), 10, 191–92, 299, 300.

entrepreneurs procured the path-breaking new laws of the 1920's, enlarging management power, the change moved rather quickly toward fresh standardization among the states; by the 1940's the "liberal" general incorporation act was the norm.[66] It was still possible, however, for the autonomy of state policy makers to create a crazy-quilt of variations. In the twentieth century this autonomy flowered especially in a confusing hodge-podge of functionless, arbitrary variations among state statutes regulating dealings in corporate securities.[67]

We might accept as normal institutional costs the diversity of corporation law which proceeded without over-all design or intention out of the different perceptions of problems and the varieties of means and situations of the separate states. Other issues—of justice and power—arose when states used their autonomy deliberately to cultivate differences in corporation law for their separate profit or to satisfy particular interests. The late nineteenth century saw the emergence of the state which by design made its law a special haven for businessmen who wanted a kind of corporate organization such as the law of most states denied them.

New Jersey's complaisant legislature launched the interstate competition for chartering business. It foreshadowed its career in 1875 by abolishing all limitations on maximum capitalization. It took the critical step, though, in 1888 when it authorized companies incorporated under its statute to hold stock in other companies; at the same time the state authorized formation of companies to do all their business outside New Jersey. In 1896 the state offered still more freedom to incorporators. In 1913 Governor Woodrow Wilson pressed through changes intended to make New Jersey's corporations less favorable to concentrated financial power. In 1917 the state sought to regain favor with promoters by returning to its older laws, though New Jersey courts trimmed the success of the maneuver by decisions which put stricter limits on management than ambitious empire builders were content to accept. Meanwhile Delaware had en-

[66] Dodd (7), 27; Hornstein (4), 1:iv, 14, 66.
[67] Loss, 1:90.

tered the competition. Already in 1899 a Delaware act followed the New Jersey original and outdid it in the scope allowed to corporate promoters. In 1915 Delaware capitalized on New Jersey's temporary retreat to strictness by a new general incorporation act, the liberality of which it enlarged in 1927 and 1929. In decisions which allowed corporation promoters and management to pursue their ends relatively free of embarrassing claims of investors, Delaware courts fully matched the indulgence which its legislature showed. In the early twentieth century other states—notably Maine and West Virginia, later Nevada —followed the models of New Jersey and Delaware, but with less success; the two originators enjoyed the prestige of innovators whose names had become associated with business of major standing and importance.[68]

The immediate interest of New Jersey and Delaware and their imitators was to obtain revenues by attracting a disproportionate amount of the business of issuing corporate charters. In this they succeeded in varying measures for varying periods of time.[69] But business ambitions supplied the underlying drive which gave the states their opportunity. At the turn of the century the prime business desire back of the New Jersey and Delaware statutes was a corporate structure which would facilitate concentration; this focus was indicated when New Jersey and Delaware removed limits on capitalization, sanctioned the holding company, and gave promoters maximum freedom to fashion patterns of bonds and shares to suit their own designs for attracting capital and appropriating their own profit. Between the 1890's and the late 1920's bigness lost its novelty and began to take on institutionalized status. Corporate insiders now showed a livelier concern to consolidate control within their empires; the Delaware acts of 1927 and 1929 gave almost unlimited power to directors vis-à-vis investors, and the notable popularity of the haven states with large public-issue corporations attested

[68] Brandeis (1), 557–64; Dodd (7), 27, 34, 43, 44, and (23), 428; Hornstein (4), 1:71–74, 80, 81, 125, 134; Jennings, (1), 195; Latty (2), 363; Stevens (1), 6, 7. *Cf.* Jennings (2), 937.

[69] Brandeis (1) 559, note 37; Hornstein (4), 1:64, 71, 74, 81–86; Rutledge, 311; Stevens (1) 6.

the importance attached to a free hand for those who sat atop broad stockholder constituencies.[70]

From the 1920's through the 1930's more and more states revised their general incorporation acts to imitate New Jersey and Delaware. The common core of this movement was delegation of broad power to the private initiators or controllers of corporate business to write charters and bylaws which gave them the structure and procedures they wanted. The common outcome for the public-issue type of company was to create and maintain domination of the corporation's affairs by an oligarchy of key directors and corporate bureaucrats. Insider control was less sharply distinguished from general investor interest in proportion as a corporation was more closely held; for such firms the new style of general incorporation statute spelled less dramatic shifts of power, but the discretion given to private draftsmen still stood in sharp contrast to the typical general laws of the late nineteenth century.[71] Though the new type of statute became the norm by mid-twentieth century, some states had been in the van of this movement, and by reason of their economies some of these were more active centers of chartering than others. By various criteria—annual lists of new corporations compiled by states by Dun and Bradstreet, lists of corporations by size of assets, listings on the New York Stock Exchange, registrations with the SEC—ten states emerged as specially important states of incorporation: California, Delaware, Illinois, Maryland, Massachusetts, Michigan, New Jersey, New York, Ohio, and Pennsylvania. There were particular concentrations of activity within the leading ten. At mid-twentieth century New York state alone accounted for almost 20 per cent of all corporations chartered in the fifty states and almost 20 per cent of the largest corporations (by size of assets) in all the states; Delaware could count a majority of all corporations among those whose shares were listed on the New York Stock Exchange or were registered

[70] Berle (8), 211; Brandeis (1), 563–65; Dodd (7), 34, and (16), 813; Hornstein (4), 1:64, 66, 69, 70–73, 80, 81; Rutledge, 312. *Cf.* Dodd (8), 290.

[71] Dodd (7), 44, and (8), 275; Hornstein (4), 1:66, 69, 72; Jennings (1), 204; Stevens (1), 6, 980.

with the SEC. As of 1956 one count showed that 498 of the 600 largest industrial, merchandising, and utility companies in the United States were incorporated in ten states.[72]

States of Incorporation of Largest Nonfinancial Corporations in 1956

		CORPORATIONS	
		Number	Assets (*millions*)
1.	Delaware	202	55,424
2.	New York	85	40,991
3.	New Jersey	45	22,768
4.	Pennsylvania	45	11,659
5.	Ohio	36	7,859
6.	Illinois	29	6,402
7.	California	13	4,864
8.	Maryland	18	3,777
9.	Indiana	11	3,528
10.	Virginia	14	2,476

SOURCE: Adapted from New York, Joint Legislative Committee to Study Revision of Corporation Laws, *Interim Report to 1957 Session of New York State Legislature,* Legislative Documents (1957), no. 17, app. D, p. 61.

Some weighty contemporary opinion and the nearly unanimous judgment of later commentators attribute to the competitive impact of New Jersey and Delaware the spread of legislation liberal in delegation of powers to corporate insiders.[73] Insofar as this is true, the outcome represents a major impact of federal institutions upon the course of corporation law. Of course, the active interest of businessmen and their lawyers supplied the impetus.[74] But the separate existence of the states, with the individual self-interest of states ready to compete for chartering business, provided an indispensable setting for this particular expression of business interest. The turn to federal se-

[72] Gibson, 296; Hornstein (4), 1:iv.

[73] See note 70 *supra; cf.* Brandeis (1), 565; Dodd (8), 275; Jennings (1), 195.

[74] Berle (2), 563, 564, and (8), 211; Hornstein (4), 1:v, 66, 119.

curities regulation in the 1930's affords circumstantial evidence of the crippling effect on independent state policy making exerted by competition among states and by the comparative weakness of individual states confronting the pressure and influence of big business. The vulnerability of the states as separate policy makers not only revealed the need of central government action to protect investors but also was a substantial factor in generating the necessary impetus to move Congress to a more positive role.[75] Of course, the states possessed formal legal authority to put some limits upon entry of foreign corporations. The Court would police against their imposition of conditions found unconstitutional as unduly burdening interstate commerce or violating standards of rationality and equality found in the Fourteenth Amendment. But by definition the ban on such unconstitutional conditions on entry did not negate the states' authority to have some say about how business was done within their borders.[76] Doctrine here had its shadows and ambiguities. But the states did not choose any such large-scale opposition to the pattern set by New Jersey and Delaware as might have provoked litigation to resolve the ambiguities of their power.

There is probably some overlap in explanation of events with the themes of the first of these essays. Attitudes toward the corporate device as such changed from generalized distrust to generalized, matter-of-fact acceptance between 1820 and 1920. The premium which prevailing social values put upon increasing productivity and entrepreneurial skill in the 1920's favored large concessions to promoters and managers. Change was in the air, was welcome because it was seen to promise growth and wealth; there was a disposition to accept legal arrangements which gave flexibility of maneuver for businessmen to use and adapt to change.[77] All this plausibly weighs in what happened. Yet the facts of federalism remain to set the scene of events.

[75] Dodd (12), 930, and (18), 274; Hornstein (4), 1:398, 428–29; Jennings (1), 196, and (2), 937, 974; Manning (1), 1486; *cf.* Loss, 1:9; Rutledge, 307, 308.

[76] Cataldo, 491; Henderson, 106–11, 142–47; Rutledge, 311.

[77] Latty (3), 609, 610, 611–12; Rutledge, 311, 312; Stevens (1), 980; see note 70, *supra*.

The separate existence of the states made itself powerfully felt in provision of new options to business ambition and in the limited practical capacity of individual state apparatus to oppose state policy to strong currents of demand from the builders of big business. So the institutional situation of the federal system shaped the role of the states and, ultimately, of the national government.

The counterpart dimension of public policy to those defined by the roles of legal agencies was the scope which corporation law gave to private will. After we take all due account of the law's restrictions, the main line of operational policy from 1780 to 1970 was to use corporation law generously to support private business organization. From 1780 to 1890 the statutes showed active concern that the corporate instrument would allow a dangerous scale of private power. Hence legislation often set limits on corporate life, purposes, and capitalization. Yet, within these limits we granted corporate status substantially to all who sought it, whether by special or general laws. Moreover, there is little evidence that the limits we set had lasting, material effect. Businessmen found legislatures ready to grant special charters on terms more to their liking than those set in the earlier, optional general incorporation statutes. When general acts—first with limiting provisions—became the exclusive avenues to incorporation about the 1870's, this limiting pattern lasted hardly twenty years before it yielded to a new style of enabling act, allowing private organizers more and more discretion to write corporate articles and bylaws to their own prescription. After 1890 the states largely stopped using the law of corporate organization as a means of regulating the impact of business organization either upon such immediately involved interests as those of shareholders or creditors or upon general social interests. In the twentieth century both state and federal law (including new federal regulations affecting corporate financial structure and corporations' market behavior) in effect accepted corporations in such sizes and shapes as businessmen could develop them. The principal reliance of the SEC-centered legislation upon disclosure as the control upon corporate power

reflected continuing acceptance of substantial corporate autonomy. This over-all march of policy was consistent with our
long-term reliance on the market as an institution of social control. Yet the growth of the practical power of large corporations
posed serious questions of the market's capacity to enforce all
relevant responsibility on private powerholders. Concern that
we were moving into grave issues on this score emerged in specialized legal regulation, focused not on corporate organization
but on particular social impacts of corporate behavior—on
labor, on consumers, on dealers, on investors, on the market.
This concern was also betrayed in brave words from the 1920's
on about the promise of corporate statesmanship and the need
for large business corporations to show their ability to be good
citizens. Such mid-twentieth-century talk had in common with
mid-nineteenth-century attacks on corporate privilege and lack
of soul, the felt presence of unresolved issues of the legitimacy
—in the sense of the responsibility—of private organized
power. In practice we continued to accept large roles for private
institutionalized power, formally legitimated through corporation law, but without clear confidence that we had reached a durable relation of such private power to the general constitutional
tradition of the society.

This inventory of the impact of public and private institutional processes upon the grounds of policy toward the business
corporation suggests how difficult it is to hold law to its proper
role as servant and not master of life. The organization and procedures of legal agencies, the structure of federalism, the inherited dignity of precedent, the inertia of familiar legal concepts
and practices, as well as our attitudes toward the market and
the proper autonomy of private will—all had effect upon the development of law affecting the business corporation. After making due allowance for the legal elements, the record as a whole
tells us that the main influences upon public policy came from
currents of life outside of and environing the formal legal system. We come back to the matter of the first two essays. What
basically shaped policy were men's ideas about productive and
acceptable ways of organizing behavior and their partly deliber-

ate, partly trial-and-error conceptions of the instruments and conditions which were functionally necessary to the kind of social patterns they trusted and wanted to adopt. The deepest roots of the law of the business corporation drew from the general life, and not just from the law.

The Social Impact of Corporation Law

THAT business corporations were important in the country's life did not prove that corporation law was; there might be a great difference in effect between going organizations and the titles, structures, and procedures with which law endowed them. At the outset, these essays noted two different estimates of the social impact of the law of business corporations. In the early twentieth century Charles W. Eliot and Nicholas Murray Butler reckoned the corporation, as the law gave it shape, the most important contrivance of their time for developing the economy. Some fifty years later Bayless Manning saw corporation law as a rusting framework through which winds of change whistled unhindered; reality lay wholly in the wills and institutional ways of businessmen. It would far exceed the bounds of these essays—not to say the available data—to attempt detailed assessment of these variant judgments. However, the essays reflect the fact that over a span of nearly two hundred years public policy paid a good deal of attention to the terms on which we would accept the corporation as a legitimate instrument of business energy and ambition. Given this record, the differences between Eliot and Butler on the one hand and Manning on the other return to provoke questions.

The Eliot-Butler–Manning difference points up the marked shift in public policy toward the business corporation which occurred between about 1890 and the 1930's. Eliot and Butler put a high rating on the social impact of corporation law because they spoke in years of major change in the law as well as of major growth in corporate business. Manning struck his appraisal in the 1960's, after a generation's stable acceptance of the enabling-act type of corporation law, which emerged as a national norm out of developments at the turn of the century.

Eliot and Butler rated high the new style of instrument which the law had just made available; Manning took it for granted, and in doing so implicitly bore witness to how integral it had become to the economy.

These commentators were not at such odds as they might appear to be, for they were talking about different things. They all addressed themselves to corporation law, but they focused on different functions of it, and the difference in focus itself reflected changing currents of policy. Butler, Eliot, and Manning all weighed the social legitimacy of corporation law. However, Butler and Eliot measured legitimacy by utility, while Manning measured it by responsibility. The first two found twentieth-century corporation law of large and good effect because it provided a useful tool for expanding economic activity and productive effort. Manning rated the same corporation law of little effect because he found that it provided scant controls over those who wielded practical power within corporate organizations. The three together were faithful to the dominant direction of policy from 1890 into the 1960's, which put the law of corporate structure at the service of top management and for social regulation turned mostly to specialized *ad hoc* standards, rules, and agencies outside the corporation.

The corporate instrument proved useful to economic growth and materially affected its character—by encouraging multiplication of ventures and by assisting the larger scale of enterprise for which technology and expanding markets supplied the prime dynamics. These propositions are plausibly established by the large currents of events, though we cannot support them out of detailed, firm-by-firm, industry-by-industry records of business decision making and business invention. Prime circumstantial evidence is the continued, increasing demands which businessmen made on law to supply them the corporate form of organization; this was a source of pressure too pragmatic to derive from other than experienced conviction of utility. Circumstantial evidence lies also in the law's own institutional responses. Our legal tradition began by regarding corporate status as uniquely created by the sovereign's action and existing strictly on the sovereign's terms. To limits set in legislation, courts added at times their own brand of doctrinal conservatism; legislatures tended to respond to practical demands with more opportunism, while courts developed more tradition of rationalizing policy and more readily fell captive to their rationalizations. Businessmen sometimes found corporation law less than fully responsive to the practical services they wanted from corporate organization. Legislative inertia held them to the cumbersome, costly procedure of obtaining desired corporate status by special charters. General and special laws set limits on corporate purpose, size, and structure. From time to time judge-made law hampered flexible use of the corporate device by insisting dogmatically upon consequences thought to follow from a corporation's nature as a formal entity which could act only according to the logic of its legal character. So by early doctrine a corporation might act with legal effect only under its seal. Decisions held corporate authority strictly to charter terms and denied the existence of flexible implied powers. In dicta even more than in decisions about the consequences of action outside formal corporate powers (*ultra vires*) judges manufactured legal uncertainties to shroud business operations. The rigor with which some courts insisted on maintaining standard forms of organization hampered adopting the corporation to the proper needs of close-held firms. Yet, on the whole, both statute and judge-made law grew in ways calculated to make the corporation a more flexible business tool. Drags derived from the law's own inertias or abstractions did not last much past the point at which businessmen began to make common and large-scale use of the corporate form. Special chartering lingered longer than it should have, but in earlier years it did point up the truly special character of public-utility-type franchises. The general incorporation acts took over the scene rapidly as general industry and commerce claimed the corporation in the last quarter of the nineteenth century; statutory limitations gave way in less than a generation from this turning point to more flexible forms. By the early nineteenth century courts relaxed their insistence on action under the corporate seal; by midcentury decisions were hospitable to finding in charters such implied powers as were necessary or proper to the corporation's business, and this development

along with broader statutory grants made obsolete a generation's ponderous learning in *ultra vires*. In mid-twentieth century the most conspicuous remaining institutional drag of law
upon the corporate instrument was the uncertainty which could
still cloud efforts to adapt the corporation to the close-held firm.
The prevailing pattern adapted corporation law to business use;
given normal institutional resistance, this adaptation moved fast
enough and on a wide enough front to attest that the corporation, as businessmen wanted it, was rated so useful as to generate specially insistent pressure that corporation law should
achieve legitimacy by realizing this utility.

If we ask more specifically what prime business utilities corporation law provided, the record of legal development and
business practice suggests two outstanding heads. For both
small and large enterprises the corporation provided a defined,
legally protected, and practically firm position of authority for
those in central control. The characteristic internal arrangement
of power differed between large and small enterprises. In the
small firm the corporate form gave power to the majority investment interest vis-à-vis the minority; in the large firm it gave
power to central decision makers (more and more without need
of substantial accompanying investment interest) vis-à-vis the
bulk of those who had capital at risk in the firm's securities.
Mechanisms differed. In the close-held firm, management held
power primarily through the combination of a voting majority
and the separation-of-powers doctrine, which left directors and
officers beyond interference by stockholders, except upon showing of gross negligence or abuse of trust. In the firm with a substantial body of shareholders, these same elements figured, but
the more immediate assurance of central control lay in the law's
sanctioning of proxy voting, coupled with management's practical control of the proxy machinery for nominating directors and
framing issues put to shareholders.

The second prime business utility provided by corporation
law was help in mustering capital. Again, the end was served
both for big and little enterprise but in different manners. One
difference affected the general pattern of firms. The corporation's capital-raising utilities encouraged multiplication of small

firms, while they helped a few enterprises achieve larger size. That the corporation allowed limited commitments figured in these outcomes but again in different ways. Limited liability of stockholders could foster investment in small ventures, but the influence of this factor was modified by the tendency of substantial creditors to insist on the personal credit of the principal investors. The corporate form distinctively helped muster capital for small firms by providing a standard format within which to combine investors active in management with investors who desired a more passive role. The corporation helped muster capital for the large firm by legitimating a flexible structure of shares and long-term debt, protecting management's discretion in retaining earnings, and providing assured limited liability for stockholders. In the large enterprise limited liability could provide an effective inducement to limited-commitment investors, because creditors had the assurance of an institutionalized pool of assets, even though they lacked practical means to exact personal responsibility from a diffuse body of capital contributors. However, we must not exaggerate the role of corporation law in mobilizing capital for the large enterprise. Essential to the outcome were the growth of the investment banking industry and the stock exchanges and later the development of institutional investors. The corporation provided the stock in trade of these institutions. But, for their part, these institutions made it possible for corporations to reach large sources of capital. Moreover, the stock market complemented the inducement of limited liability by offering the investor practical options to move in and out of commitments.

To say that corporation law helped multiply enterprises and helped technology and business ambition create a larger scale of firm is not to say that the particular corporation law we had was indispensable to these outcomes. United States economic history shows too much ingenious improvising, too much restless energy, to make such a thesis plausible. However, it would be equally unreal to conclude that because it was not indispensable the corporation law we had was unimportant to these business outcomes. The functional needs to be served were there—the need of a workable internal division of powers within business organizations, the need to attract capital with appeals varied according to scale and risk and investors' goals. Had we devised some different legal format to serve these needs, the underlying business drives would have required that the other form of organization in working substance must resemble the corporation. The point is supported by what English businessmen and lawyers did in the eighteenth and early nineteenth centuries in developing the joint stock company under deed of settlement, as a functional counterpart of the corporation.

Through most of the nineteenth century corporation law embodied formal efforts to impose social responsibility upon corporate enterprise as well as to provide incorporation as a business utility. One dimension of responsibility was to utility itself. To hold the corporation responsible to fulfill its immediate economic functions, the law gave certain rights to creditors and stockholders and, in effect, trusted their self-interest to attend to the general social interest that the corporate firm behave as a productive entity in market. Thus, creditors would police the integrity of the corporation as a separate working capital fund, and stockholders would hold directors and officers to standards of fidelity and care in operations. There are no inventories to measure how much impact creditor and stockholder surveillance had. But the formal record is sparse and episodic enough to suggest that creditor and stockholder safeguards built into corporation law at least lacked steady effect to enforce the immediate utility criterion of legitimacy. Creditor issues over the corporate "trust fund' typically arose only at points of major breakdown. The stockholder's vote seems likely always to have had limited effect in firms of any size, and the weaknesses of the stockholder's derivative suit were persistent. After 1890 the main trends of the statutes further reduced the opportunity of creditors or stockholders to police corporate legitimacy through provisions embodied in corporate structure itself. Twentieth-century corporation statutes paid little specialized attention to creditor interests and, in effect, remitted creditors for protection to their own zeal and ingenuity through the law of contract and the machinery of credit ratings and information. The standard twentieth-century corporation statute put such broad discretion in those controlling corporate enterprise—to design articles and bylaws, to shape the financial structure, to control directors' and officers' tenure through the proxy machinery, and to enjoy substantial autonomy in regular operating decisions—as to reduce the general stockholder electorate to a quite residual control function, wielded more through shares trading and take-over threats than through processes set up in the law of corporate organization itself. As individuals or small groups, stockholders still held the disciplinary threat of suits for the corporation's benefit against faithless or careless directors or officers. Yet legislation in some states materially curbed this remedy, and in any case there remained stubborn practical difficulties—costs and risks of suit, lack of information, want of incentive in terms of return to the individual suitors—which sharply limited resort to the remedy.

To the end of the nineteenth century corporation law often built some regulations into corporate structure to protect general social interests. The statutes did this especially to protect the market as an institution of social control, to this end setting limits on corporate purposes, duration, and size. There is little evidence that these limitations substantially affected business behavior. Special charters often avoided limits put into optional general incorporation acts, and where limits were set, they were not infrequently amended out of existence. By the time the general incorporation act became the exclusive avenue to corporate status, such limits were being relaxed. Insofar as formal restrictions continued, they were rarely enforced. The state might on writ of *quo warranto* seek to withdraw a corporate franchise for abuse of its terms. But this remedy was so drastic that it was not used. Under inherited Equity powers, courts might conceivably entertain suits to enjoin charter violations. But initiative here lay with jacks-of-all-trades public prosecutors, who had little incentive to move in such matters compared with the flow of more ordinary law enforcement business pressing on them. Such public action as was taken through the courts usually focused, not on violations of the terms set for corporate status, but on violations of conditions set for special-action franchises of public utilities. Thus, when it became standard in the early twentieth century to drop from the general corporation statutes regulations primarily directed at general social interests, the change simply made form fit existing substance. In this light Manning's judgment of the lack of general regulatory impact in corporation law of the 1960's is valid, but the fact does not represent a material change from the situation as it had existed, at least since use of the corporate device became widespread in the late nineteenth century.

These developments implied two judgments on problems of social process—one concerning ends, the other means. As to ends: We gave up building general social controls into corporate structure in the first instance by legislative response to the pressures of businessmen that corporation law serve simply the utility function, providing them a ready instrument to muster capital and put it under assumed central direction. But this approach—at first taken in a handful of states moved also by their own greed for revenue—broadened into a national norm. That it did so suggested prevailing acceptance of, or at least acquiescence in, the idea that the corporation's utility served the general economy as well as more specific interests. But this direction of policy carried another suggestion. We also ceased to build general social controls into corporate structure because the large business corporation grew to involve a wider range of interests than the corporation's own internal constitution could mediate; hence, the law moved into an expanding variety of specific subjectmatter regulations which, though not formally so limited, in fact mainly concerned adjustment of social interests affected by large corporation behavior.

The trend of policy also implied a judgment on methods of legal regulation in an economy in which large-scale firms were the most influential private decision makers. Experience indicated that nothing short of specialized, continuous executive or administrative attention would supply significant external checks on the responsibility of those who held central power in corporations with large numbers of shareholders. In particular we saw increased surveillance of corporate financial practices through the stock exchanges and the SEC and through a new body of case law built by federal courts on the foundation of the SEC statutes and SEC regulations. These developments materially affected an important range of corporate decision making. Notably, they spelled the growth of important checks on those who controlled corporations by authority outside the frame of the corporation. Most stock exchange and SEC regulation, as well as the new law of the federal courts, formally sought to energize traditional stockholder checks on management. But the main practical impact was from what the stock exchange or the SEC or the courts did rather than from what stockholders did.

However, these new regulations centered simply on corporate finance. As large corporations increased the range of their impact on society, a wider spread of problems challenged public policy processes—concerning the market as an institution of social control, concerning diffuse public interests in natural resource conservation and in public health and safety, and concerning important interests (those of labor, dealers and suppliers, and consumers) outside the formal structure of the corporation but affected in more focused ways by what the corporation did. In mid-twentieth century public policy made fumbling response to the reality of the broadened impact of the big corporation through specialized federal and state regulatory laws put in charge of specialized executive or administrative offices. There was gathering concern, however, that this drift of events evaded issues basic to the working constitution of this society. Policy making needed the knowledge, experience, and sustained follow-through which specialized executive, or administrative effort, could supply. But we put more of a load on executive, or administrative, offices than they could carry politically when we assigned to them as much responsibility for defining and ordering values involved with large-scale corporate business as we did through the first three-quarters of the twentieth century. Thus, in 1970, somewhat as in the 1880's, we had reached an apparent equilibrium of policy in law concerning corporations, but it seemed likely to prove as unstable an equilibrium as that of the 1880's. For all the brave talk of a new stockholder democracy and a new corporate statesmanship, it was unlikely that we would find satisfactory adjustment of the large corporation to the social context through new controls built into the corporation's own constitution; this aspect of legal development since 1890 would likely endure. But there would be insistent continuing demand to legitimize corporation power by its responsibility as well as its utility. To this end we would ultimately require a more comprehensive legislative response than any we had achieved by 1970.

Bibliography

Adler, Mortimer, and Louis O. Kelso. *The Capitalist Manifesto.* New York: Random House, 1958.

Allen, Frederick Lewis. *The Big Change: America Tranforms Itself, 1900–1950.* New York: Harper & Bros., 1952.

Ames, Samuel. See Angell and Ames.

Angell, Joseph K., and Samuel Ames. *Treatise on the Law of Private Corporations Aggregate.* Boston: Little and Brown, 1832.

Aranow, Edward Ross, and Herbert A. Einhorn. *Proxy Contests for Corporate Control.* New York: Columbia University Press, 1957.

Baker, Ralph, and William L. Cary. *Corporations: Cases and Materials.* 3d ed., abr. Brooklyn: Foundation Press, 1959.

Ballentine, Arthur. *Ballentine on Corporations.* rev. ed. Chicago: Callaghan & Co., 1946.

Baum, Daniel Jay, and Ned B. Stiles. *The Silent Partners: Institutional Investors and Corporate Control.* Syracuse, N.Y.: Syracuse University Press, 1965.

Bayne, David C., Mortimer Caplin, Frank D. Emerson, and Franklin C. Latcham. "Proxy Regulations and the Rule-Making Process: The 1954 Amendments." 40 *Va. L. Rev.* 387 (1954).

Bazelon, David T. *The Paper Economy.* New York: Vintage Books, 1965.

Beard, Charles A., and Mary Beard. *The Rise of American Civilization.* New York: Macmillan, 1927.

Berle, Adolph A., Jr.
  (1) *Studies in the Law of Corporation Finance.* Chicago: Callaghan & Co., 1928.
  (2) "Investors and the Revised Delaware Corporation Act." 29 *Colum. L. Rev.* 563 (1929).
  (3) "Corporate Powers as Powers in Trust." 44 *Harv. L. Rev.* 1049 (1931).

(4) "For Whom Corporate Managers *Are* Trustees." 45 *Harv. L. Rev.* 1365 (1932).

(5) Foreword to Elvin R. Latty. *Subsidiaries and Affiliated Corporations*. Chicago: Foundation Press, Inc., 1936.

(6) "Stock Market Manipulation." 38 *Colum. L. Rev.* 393 (1938).

(7) Book review: Stevens, *Handbook on the Law of Corporations*. 2d ed. 35 *Cornell L.Q.* 249 (1949).

(8) "Historical Inheritance of American Corporations." In *The Powers and Duties of Corporate Management,* edited by Edmund Cahn. Social Meaning of Legal Concepts Series. New York: New York University Law Center, 1950.

(9) Book review: Hugh L. Soward, *Cases, Comments and Materials on Corporation Finance*. 26 *N.Y.U.L.Q.* 235 (1951).

(10) "Constitutional Limitations on Corporate Activity: Protection of Personal Rights from Invasion through Economic Power." 100 *U. Pa. L. Rev.* 933 (1952).

(11) *The 20th Century Capitalist Revolution.* New York: Harcourt, Brace & Co., 1954.

(12) Book review: Stevens and Larson, *Cases and Materials on the Law of Corporations*. 2d ed. 41 *Cornell L.Q.* 336 (1955).

(13) " 'Control' in Corporate Law." 58 *Colum. L. Rev.* 1212 (1958).

(14) *Power Without Property: A New Development in American Political Economy*. New York: Harcourt, Brace & Co., 1959.

(15) *The Corporation and the Economy*. Santa Barbara, Calif.: Center for the Study of Democratic Institutions, 1959.

(16) "Legal Problems of Economic Power." 60 *Colum. L. Rev.* 4 (1960).

(17) Book review: Hornstein, *Business Corporation Law and Practice*. 74 *Harv. L. Rev.* 428 (1960).

(18) "Modern Functions of the Corporate System." 62 *Colum. L. Rev.* 433 (1962).

(19) "Economic Power and the Free Society," In *Corporation Takeover,* edited by Andrew Hacker. New York: Harper & Row, 1964.

(20) "Property, Production and Revolution." 65 *Colum. L. Rev.* 1 (1965).

Berle, Adolph A., Jr., and Gardiner C. Means. *The Modern Corporation and Private Property.* New York: The Macmillan Co., 1933.

Berle, Adolph A., Jr., and Victoria J. Pederson. *Liquid Claims and National Wealth.* New York: The Macmillan Co., 1934.

Blum, Walter J. "The Law and Language of Corporate Reorganization." 17 *U. Chi. L. Rev.* 565 (1950).

Bowen, Howard R. *Social Responsibilities of the Businessman.* New York: Harper & Bros., 1953.

Brandeis, Louis D.
   (1) Dissent, Liggett v. Lee, 288 U.S. 517, 541 (1933).
   (2) Unpublished dissenting opinion in Stratton v. St. Louis Southwestern Railway Co. (1929). In Alexander M. Bickel, *The Unpublished Opinions of Mr. Justice Brandeis: The Supreme Court at Work.* Cambridge, Mass.: Harvard University Press, Belknap Press, 1957.

Broude, Henry W. "The Role of the State in American Economic Development, 1820–1890." In Committee on Economic Growth, *The State and Economic Growth.* New York: Social Science Research Council, 1959.

Bruchey, Stuart. *The Roots of American Growth, 1607–1861: An Essay in Social Causation.* New York: Harper & Row, Harper Torchbooks, 1968.

Buchanan, Norman S. *The Economics of Corporate Enterprise.* New York: Henry Holt & Co., 1940.

Bunn, Charles W., ed. *A Brief Survey of the Jurisdiction and Practice of the Courts of the United States.* 4th ed. St. Paul: West Publishing Co., 1949.

Byrne, James. "The Foreclosure of Railroad Mortgages in the United States Courts." In Association of the Bar of the City of New York, *Some Legal Phases of Corporate Financing, Reorganization and Regulation.* New York: Macmillan Co., 1930.

Cadman, John W., Jr. *The Corporation in New Jersey: Business and Politics, 1791–1875.* Cambridge, Mass.: Harvard University Press, 1949.

Caplin, Mortimer M. "Proxies, Annual Meetings and Corporate Democracy: The Lawyer's Role." 37 *Va. L. Rev.* 653 (1951). See also Bayne, Caplin, Emerson, and Latcham.

Carnegie, Andrew. "Wealth and Its Uses." In Louis M. Hacker and Helene S. Zahler, *The Shaping of the American Tradition.* 2 vols. 2:807. New York: Columbia University Press, 1947.

Cary, William L. See Baker and Cary.

Cataldo, Bernard F. "Limited Liability with One-Man Companies and Subsidiary Corporations." 18 *Law & Contemp. Prob.* 473 (1953).

Chandler, Alfred D., Jr.
  (1) "Henry Varnum Poor: Philosopher of Management, 1812–1905." In *Men in Business,* edited by William Miller, p. 254. Cambridge, Mass.: Harvard University Press, 1955.
  (2) *Strategy and Structure: Chapters in the History of the Industrial Enterprise.* Cambridge, Mass.: M.I.T. Press, 1962.

Chayes, Abram. "The Modern Corporation and the Rule of Law." In *The Corporation in Modern Society,* edited by Edward S. Mason, p. 25. Cambridge, Mass.: Harvard University Press, 1960.

Cochran, Thomas C.
  (1) *Railroad Leaders, 1845–1890: The Business Mind in Action.* Cambridge, Mass.: Harvard University Press, 1953.
  (2) "The Entrepreneur in American Capital Formation." In National Bureau of Economic Research, *Capital Formation and Economic Growth,* p. 339. Princeton, N.J.: Princeton University Press, 1955.
  (3) "Did the Civil War Retard Industrialization?" In *The Economic Impact of the American Civil War,* edited by Ralph Andreano, p. 148. Cambridge, Mass.: Schenkman Publishing Co., 1962.

Cochran, Thomas C., and William Miller. *The Age of Enterprise: A Social History of Industrial America.* New York: Macmillan Co., 1943.

Cooke, C. A. *Corporation Trust and Company.* Cambridge, Mass.: Harvard University Press, 1951.

Dahl, Robert A., and Charles E. Lindblom. *Politics, Economics, and Welfare.* New York: Harper & Brothers., 1953.

Davis, Joseph S. *Essays in the Earlier History of American Corporations.* 2 vols. Cambridge, Mass.: Harvard University Press, 1917.

Dean, Arthur H. "Twenty-Five Years of Federal Securities Regulation by the Securities and Exchange Commission." 59 *Colum. L. Rev.* 697 (1959).

de Capriles, Miguel. "Fifteen-Year Survey of Corporate Developments, 1944–1959." 13 *Vand. L. Rev.* 1 (1959).

Dewing, Arthur Stone. *The Financial Policy of Corporations.* 4th ed. 2 vols. New York: Ronald Press, 1941.

Director, Aaron. "The Modern Corporation and the Control of Property." In *Conference on Corporation Law and Finance*. Conference Series no. 8. Chicago: Law School, University of Chicago, 1951.

Dodd, E. Merrick, Jr.

(1) "Dissenting Stockholders and Amendments to Corporate Charters." 75 *U. Pa. L. Rev.* 585 (1927).

(2) "Dogma and Practice in the Law of Associations." 42 *Harv. L. Rev.* 977 (1929).

(3) "For Whom Are Corporate Managers Trustees?" 45 *Harv. L. Rev. 1145* (1932).

(4) Book review: Berle and Means, *The Modern Corporation and Private Property*. 81 *U. Pa. L. Rev.* 782 (1933).

(5) "How Not to Amend the Federal Securities Act: Fundamental Purpose Should Not be Impaired." 20 *A.B.A.J.* 247 (1934).

(6) "Amending the Securities Act: The ABA Committee's Proposals." 45 *Yale L. J.* 199 (1935).

(7) "Statutory Developments in Business Corporation Law, 1886–1936." 50 *Harv. L. Rev.* 27 (1936).

(8) "American Business Association Law a Hundred Years Ago and Today." In *LAW: A Century of Progress, 1835–1935*. 3 vols. 3:254. New York: New York University Press, 1937.

(9) "The Securities and Exchange Commission's Reform Program for Bankruptcy Reorganization." 38 *Colum. L. Rev.* 223 (1938).

(10) *Lectures on the Growth of Corporate Structure in the United States with Special Reference to Governmental Regulations*. Cleveland: Cleveland Bar Association, 1938.

(11) Book review: Livermore, *Early American Land Companies*. 40 *Colum. L. Rev.* 356 (1940).

(12) "The Modern Corporation, Private Property, and Recent Federal Legislation." 54 *Harv. L. Rev.* 917 (1941).

(13) "Purchase and Redemption by a Corporation of Its Own Shares: The Substantive Law." 89 *U. Pa. L. Rev.* 697 (1941).

(14) "Investor Protection by Administrative Agency: The United States Securities and Exchange Commission." 5 *Mod. L. Rev.* 174 (1942).

(15) Book review: Cherington, *The Investor and the Securities Act*. 43 *Colum. L. Rev.* 139 (1943).

(16) Book review: *Federal Corporation Act: Preliminary Draft Prepared by the Corporation Law Committee of the American Bar Association.* 53 *Yale L. J.* 812 (1944).

(17) Book review: *Report of the Committee on Company Law Amendment.* 58 *Harv. L. Rev.* 1258 (1945).

(18) "The United States Securities and Exchange Commission: 1942–1946." 10 *Mod. L. Rev.* 255 (1947).

(19) Book review: Ballentine, *Corporations.* rev. ed. 60 *Harv. L. Rev.* 1006 (1947).

(20) Book review: Handlins, *Commonwealth: Massachusetts.* 61 *Harv. L. Rev.* 555 (1948).

(21) Book review: Cadman, *The Corporation in New Jersey.* 63 *Harv. L. Rev.* 1478 (1950).

(22) Book review: Levy, *Private Corporations and Their Control.* 64 *Harv. L. Rev.* 526 (1951).

(23) *American Business Corporations until 1860.* Cambridge, Mass.: Harvard University Press, 1954.

Dorfman, Joseph. *The Economic Mind in American Civilization.* 5 vols. New York: Viking Press, 1949.

Drucker, Peter F.

(1) *The Future of Industrial Man: A Conservative Approach.* New York: John Day Co., 1942.

(2) *Concept of the Corporation.* New York: John Day Co., 1946.

(3) *The New Society: The Anatomy of the Industrial Order.* New York: Harper & Bros., 1949.

(4) *The Practice of Management.* New York: Harper & Bros., 1954.

Eells, Richard

(1) *The Meaning of Modern Business: An Introduction to the Philosophy of Large Corporate Enterprise.* New York: Columbia University Press, 1960.

(2) *The Government of Corporations.* New York: Free Press of Glencoe, Ill., 1962.

Einaudi, Mario. *The Roosevelt Revolution.* New York: Harcourt, Brace & Co., 1959.

Einhorn, Herbert A. See Aranow and Einhorn.

Emerson, Frank D., and Franklin C. Latcham. *Shareholder Democracy.* Cleveland: Press of Western Reserve University, 1954. See also Bayne, Caplin, Emerson, and Latcham.

Evans, George Heberton, Jr. *Business Incorporation in the United States, 1800–1943.* New York: National Bureau of Economic Research, Inc., 1948.

Finletter, Thomas K. *The Law of Bankruptcy Reorganization.* Charlottesville, Va.: Michie Co., 1939.

Fleischer, Arthur, Jr. " 'Federal Corporation Law': An Assessment." 78 *Harv. L. Rev.* 1146 (1966).

Fortune, Editors of. *The Executive Life.* New York: Doubleday & Co., Inc., 1956.

Frampton, George T. "Indemnification of Insiders Litigation Expenses." 23 *Law & Contemp. Prob.* 325 (1958).

Frankfurter, Felix. *The Public and Its Government,* New Haven: Yale University Press, 1930.

Freund, Ernst. *Standards of American Legislation.* Chicago: University of Chicago Press, 1917.

Garrett, Ray. "Attitudes on Corporate Democracy: A Critical Analysis." 51 *Nw. U.L. Rev.* 310 (1956).

Garrison, Lloyd K. Comment on Drucker. In *The Powers and Duties of Corporate Management,* edited by Edmund Cahn. Social Meaning of Legal Concepts, no. 3. New York: New York University School of Law, 1950.

Gibson, George D. "How Fixed Are Class Shareholder Rights?" 23 *Law & Contemp. Prob.* 283 (1958).

Glaeser, Martin. *Public Utilities in American Capitalism.* New York: Macmillan Co., 1957.

Goebel, Julius, Jr. Introduction to Livermore, *Early American Land Companies.* New York: The Commonwealth Fund, 1939.

Goldsmith, Raymond W. "Financial Structure and Economic Growth in Advanced Countries: An Experiment in Comparative Financial Morphology." In National Bureau of Economic Research, *Capital Formation and Economic Growth.* Princeton, N.J.: Princeton University Press, 1955.

Goodrich, Carter. *Government Promotion of American Canals and Railroads, 1800–1890.* New York: Columbia University Press, 1960.

Gordon, Robert A. *Business Leadership in the Large Corporation.* Washington, D.C.: Brookings Institution, 1945.

Gouge, William M. *Short History of Paper Money and Banking in the United States.* 2d ed. New York: B. & S. Collins, 1835.

Govan, Thomas Payne. *Nicholas Biddle: Nationalist and Public Banker, 1786–1844.* Chicago: University of Chicago Press, 1959.

Gower, L. C. B.
  (1) "The English Private Company." 18 *Law & Contemp. Prob.*
      535 (1953).
  (2) "Some Contrasts between British and American Corpora-
      tion Law." 69 *Harv. L. Rev.* 1369 (1956).
Graham, Benjamin. *The Intelligent Investor.* New York: Harper &
  Bros., 1949.
Graham, Howard Jay. *Everyman's Constitution: Historical Essays
  on the Fourteenth Amendment, the "Conspiracy Theory," and
  American Constitutionalism.* Madison, Wis.: State Historical So-
  ciety of Wisconsin, 1968.
Gregg, Dorothy. "John Stevens: General Entrepreneur, 1749–1838."
  In *Men in Business,* edited by William Miller. Cambridge, Mass.:
  Harvard University Press, 1952.
Hacker, Louis M. *The World of Andrew Carnegie: 1865–1901.*
  Philadelphia and New York: J. B. Lippincott Co., 1968.
Hacker, Louis M., and Helene S. Zahler. *The United States in the
  20th Century.* New York: Appleton-Century-Crofts, Inc., 1952.
Haines, Charles Grove. "The History of Due Process of Law after
  the Civil War." 3 *Texas L. Rev.* 1 (1924). Also in *Select Essays
  on Constitutional Law.* 3 vols. 1:268. Chicago: Association of
  American Law Schools, 1938.
Hammond, Bray. *Banks and Politics in America from the Revolu-
  tion to the Civil War.* Princeton, N.J.: Princeton University Press,
  1957.
Handlin, Oscar, and Mary Flug Handlin. *Commonwealth: A Study
  of the Role of Government in the American Economy: Massachu-
  setts, 1774–1861.* rev. ed. Cambridge, Mass.: Harvard University
  Press, 1969.
Harbrecht, Paul P. *Pension Funds and Economic Power.* New York:
  Twentieth Century Fund, 1959.
Harris, Benjamin, Jr. "The Model Business Corporation Act: Invitation to Irresponsibility?" 50 *Nw. U.L. Rev.* 1 (1955).
Harris, Seymour E. See Sutton, Harris, Kaysen, and Tobin.
Hartz, Louis
  (1) *Economic Policy and Democratic Thought: Pennsylvania,
      1776–1860.* Cambridge, Mass.: Harvard University Press,
      1948.
  (2) *The Liberal Tradition in America: An Interpretation of
      American Political Thought since the Revolution.* New
      York: Harcourt, Brace & Co., 1955.

Heath, Milton Sydney. *Constructive Liberalism: The Role of the State in Economic Development in Georgia to 1860.* Cambridge, Mass.: Harvard University Press, 1954.

Heflebower, R. B. "Conscious Parallelism and Administered Prices." In *Perspectives on Antitrust Policy,* edited by Almarin Phillips, p. 88. Princeton, N. J.: Princeton University Press, 1965.

Heller, Harry. " 'Integration' of the Dissemination of Information under the Securities Act of 1933 and the Securities Exchange Act of 1934." 29 *Law & Contemp. Prob.* 749 (1964).

Henderson, Gerard Carl. *The Position of Foreign Corporations in American Constitutional Law.* Cambridge, Mass.: Harvard University Press, 1918.

Henn, Harry G. "The Philosophies of the New York Business Corporation Law of 1961." 11 *Buffalo L. Rev.* 439 (1962).

Hetherington, J. A. C. "Trends in Legislation for Close Corporations." 1963 *Wis. L. Rev.* 92.

Hibbard, Benjamin Horace. *A History of the Public Land Policies.* Foreword by Paul W. Gates. Madison and Milwaukee: University of Wisconsin Press, 1965.

Hill, Frank Ernest. See Nevins and Hill.

Hofstadter, Richard. *The American Political Tradition and the Men Who Made It.* New York: Alfred A. Knopf, 1948.

Holmes, Oliver Wendell, Jr. "Law and the Court." In *Speeches,* p. 98. Boston: Little, Brown & Co., 1918. Also in *The Occasional Speeches of Justice Oliver Wendell Holmes,* compiled by Mark DeWolfe Howe, p. 168. Cambridge, Mass.: Harvard University Press, Belknap Press, 1962.

Hoover, Calvin B. *The Economy, Liberty, and the State.* New York: Century Fund, 1959.

Hornstein, George David
    (1) "The Death Knell of Stockholders' Derivative Suits in New York." 32 *Calif. L. Rev.* 123 (1944).
    (2) "New Aspects of Stockholders Derivative Suits." 47 *Colum. L. Rev.* 1 (1947).
    (3) "Judicial Tolerance of the Incorporated Partnership." 18 *Law & Contemp. Prob.* 435 (1953).
    (4) *Corporation Law and Practice.* 2 vols. St. Paul: West Publishing Co., 1959.

Howe, Mark DeWolfe. *The Garden and the Wilderness: Religion and Government in American Constitutional History.* Chicago: University of Chicago Press, Phoenix Books, 1967.

Hunt, Freeman. *Lives of American Merchants.* 2 vols. New York: Derby & Jackson, 1858.

Hunt, Robert S. *Law and Locomotives: The Impact of the Railroad on Wisconsin Law in the Nineteenth Century.* Madison, Wis.: State Historical Society of Wisconsin, 1958.

Hurff, George. *Social Aspects of Enterprise.* Philadelphia: University of Pennsylvania Press, 1950.

Hurst, James Willard
   (1) *The Growth of American Law: The Law Makers.* Boston: Little, Brown & Co., 1950.
   (2) *Law and the Conditions of Freedom in the Nineteenth-Century United States.* Madison, Wis.: University of Wisconsin Press, 1956.
   (3) *Law and Social Process in United States History.* Ann Arbor, Mich.: University of Michigan Law School, 1960.
   (4) *Law and Economic Growth: The Legal History of the Lumber Industry in Wisconsin, 1836–1915.* Cambridge, Mass.: Harvard University Press, Belknap Press, 1964.

Jefferson, Thomas. "First Inaugural Address, 1801." In *A Compilation of the Messages and Papers of the Presidents, 1789–1897,* edited by James D. Richardson. 20 vols. 1:321. Washington, D.C.: Government Printing Office, 1896.

Jennings, Richard W.
   (1) "The Role of the States in Corporate Regulation and Investor Protection." 23 *Law & Contemp. Prob.* 193 (1958).
   (2) "Mr. Justice Douglas: His Influence on Corporate and Securities Regulation." 73 *Yale L.J.* 920 (1964).

Johnson, E. A. J., and Herman E. Krooss. *The Origins and Development of the American Economy.* New York: Prentice-Hall, Inc., 1953.

Katz, Wilber G. "The Philosophy of Midcentury Corporation Statutes." 23 *Law & Contemp. Prob.* 177 (1958).

Kaysen, Carl, and Donald F. Turner. *Antitrust Policy: An Economic and Legal Analysis.* Cambridge, Mass.: Harvard University Press, 1965. See also Sutton, Harris, Kaysen, and Tobin.

Kelso, Louis O. See Adler and Kelso.

Kessler, Robert A. "The Statutory Requirement of a Board of Directors: A Corporate Anachronism." 27 *U. Chi. L. Rev.* 696 (1960).

Kimball, Spencer L. *Insurance and Public Policy: A Study in the*

Legal Implementation of Social and Economic Public Policy, Based on Wisconsin Records, 1835–1959. Madison, Wis.: University of Wisconsin Press, 1960.

Kirkland, Edward Chase. *Men, Cities, and Transportation: A Study in New England History, 1820–1900.* 2 vols. Cambridge, Mass.: Harvard University Press, 1948.

Knauss, Robert L. "A Reappraisal of the Role of Disclosure." 62 *Mich. L. Rev.* 607 (1964).

Knauth, Oswald. *Managerial Enterprise.* New York: W. W. Norton & Co., Inc., 1948.

Knight, Frank H. *On the History and Method of Economics: Selected Essays.* Chicago: University of Chicago Press, 1956.

Kramer, Robert. "Foreword to the Close Corporation." 18 *Law & Contemp. Prob.* 433 (1953).

Krooss, Herman E. *American Economic Development.* Englewood Cliffs, N.J.: Prentice-Hall, Inc. 1955. See also Johnson and Krooss.

Kuehnl, George J. *The Wisconsin Business Corporation.* Madison, Wis.: University of Wisconsin Press, 1959.

Kuznets, Simon. "International Differences in Capital Formation and Financing." In National Bureau of Economic Research, *Capital Formation and Economic Growth,* p. 19. Princeton, N.J.: Princeton University Press, 1955.

Kyd, Stewart. *A Treatise on the Law of Corporations.* 2 vols. London: J. Butterworth, 1794.

Larner, Robert J. "Separation of Ownership and Control and Its Implications for the Behavior of the Firm." Ph.D. dissertation, University of Wisconsin, 1968.

Latcham, Franklin C. See Bayne, Caplin, Emerson, and Latcham; Emerson and Latcham.

Latty, Elvin R.
  (1) *Subsidiaries and Affiliated Corporations.* Chicago: Foundation Press, 1936.
  (2) "Some Miscellaneous Novelties in the New Corporation Statutes." 23 *Law & Contemp. Prob.* 363 (1958).
  (3) "Some General Observations on the New Business Corporations Laws of New York." 11 *Buffalo L. Rev.* 591 (1962).

Lerner, Max. *America as a Civilization.* New York: Simon & Schuster, 1957.

Lindblom, Charles E. See Dahl and Lindblom.

Lintner, John. "The Financing of Corporations." In *The Corporation in Modern Society,* edited by Edward S. Mason, p. 166. Cambridge, Mass.: Harvard University Press, 1960.

Livermore, Shaw. *Early American Land Companies.* New York: Commonwealth Fund, 1939.

Livingston, J. A. *The American Stockholder.* rev. ed. New York: Collier Books, 1963.

Locke, John. *The Second Treatise of Civil Government and a Letter Concerning Toleration.* Edited by J. W. Gough. Oxford: B. Blackwell, 1946.

Lodge, Henry Cabot, ed. *The Federalist: A Commentary on the Constitution of the United States.* New York: G. P. Putnam's Sons, 1888.

Loss, Louis. *Securities Regulation,* 2d ed. 3 vols. Boston: Little, Brown & Co., 1961.

McCarroll, John C. See von Mehren and McCarroll.

McCloskey, Robert G. *The American Supreme Court.* Chicago: University of Chicago Press, 1960.

McConnell, Grant. *The Decline of Agrarian Democracy.* Berkeley and Los Angeles: University of California Press, 1953.

Manne, Henry G.
  (1) "The 'Higher Criticism' of the Modern Corporation." 62 *Colum. L. Rev.* 399 (1962).
  (2) "Some Theoretical Aspects of Share Voting." 64 *Colum. L. Rev.* 1427 (1964).
  (3) Book review: Berle, *The American Economic Republic.* 62 *Mich. L. Rev.* 547 (1964).
  (4) "Mergers and the Market for Corporate Control." 73 *J. Pol. Econ.* 110 (1965).

Manning, Bayless
  (1) Book review: Livingston, *The American Stockholder.* 67 *Yale L.J.* 1477 (1958).
  (2) "Corporate Power and Individual Freedom: Some General Analysis and Particular Reservations." 55 *Nw. U.L. Rev.* 55 (1960).
  (3) "The Shareholder's Appraisal Remedy." 72 *Yale L.J.* 223 (1962).

Mason, Edward S.
  (1) *Economic Concentration and the Monopoly Problem.* Cambridge, Mass.: Harvard University Press, 1957.

(2) Ed., *The Corporation in Modern Society*. Cambridge, Mass.:
Harvard University Press, 1960.

Maurer, Herryman. *Great Enterprise*. New York: The Macmillan
Co., 1955.

Means, Gardiner C. *The Corporate Revolution in America*. New
York: Collier Books, 1964. See also Berle and Means.

Meyers, Marvin. *The Jacksonian Persuasion: Politics and Belief*.
Stanford, Calif.: Stanford University Press, 1957.

Miller, William. "Business Corporations in Pennsylvania, 1800–
1860." 55 *Q. J. Econ.* 50 (1940). See also Cochran and Miller.

Mitchell, Broadus. *Alexander Hamilton: Youth to Maturity, 1755–
1788*. New York: Macmillan Co., 1957.

Moore, Wilbert E. *The Conduct of the Corporation*. New York:
Random House, 1962.

Nevins, Allan, and Frank Ernest Hill. *Ford: Expansion and Challenge, 1915–1933*. New York: Charles Scribner's Sons, New
York: 1957.

New York. *Debates and Proceedings in the New York State Convention for the Revision of the Constitution*, Albany, 1846. As
extracted in Louis M. Hacker and Helene S. Zahler, *The Shaping
of the American Tradition*, 1:515–24. New York: Columbia
University Press, 1947.

North, Douglass C. *Growth and Welfare in the American Past*.
Englewood Cliffs, N.J.: Prentice-Hall, Inc., 1966.

O'Neal, F. Hodge. *Close Corporations: Law and Practice*. 2 vols.
Chicago: Callaghan & Co., 1958.

Paul, Arnold M. *Conservative Crisis and the Rule of Law*. Ithaca,
N. Y.: Cornell University Press, 1960.

Pederson, Victoria J. See Berle and Pederson.

Peterson, Merrill D. *The Jefferson Image in the American Mind*.
New York: Oxford University Press, 1960.

Plumb, J. H. *The Growth of Political Stability in England, 1675–
1725*. London: Macmillan Co., 1967.

Polanyi, Karl. *The Great Transformation*. New York: Farrar &
Rinehart, Inc., 1944.

Pound, Roscoe

(1) *An Introduction to the Philosophy of Law*. New Haven:
Yale University Press, 1922.

(2) *The Formative Era of American Law*. Boston: Little, Brown
& Co., 1938.

Primm, James Neal. *Economic Policy in the Development of a Western State: Missouri, 1820–1860*. Cambridge, Mass.: Harvard University Press, 1954.

Prothro, James Warren, *The Dollar Decade: Business Ideas in the 1920's*. Baton Rouge, La.: Louisiana State University Press, 1954.

Radin, Max. *Manners and Morals of Business*. Indianapolis: Bobbs-Merrill Co., 1939.

Reagan, Michael D. *The Managed Economy*. New York: Oxford University Press, 1963.

Redlich, Fritz. *The Moulding of American Banking: Men and Ideas*. 2 vols. New York: Hafner Publishing Co., Inc., 1947.

Reynolds, A. R. *The Daniel Shaw Lumber Company: A Case Study of the Wisconsin Lumbering Frontier*. New York: New York University Press, 1957.

Robbins, James B. "The Private Corporation: Its Constitutional Genesis." 28 *Geo. L. Review*. 165 (1929).

Robbins, Sidney. *The Securities Markets*. New York: Free Press of Glencoe, Ill., 1966.

Rohrlich, Chester. "Initial Capitalization and Financing of Corporations." 13 *Vand. L. Rev*. 197 (1959).

Rostow, Eugene V.
   (1) *Planning for Freedom: The Public Law of American Capitalism*. New Haven: Yale University Press, 1959.
   (2) "To Whom and for What Ends Is Corporate Management Responsible?" In *The Corporation in Modern Society*, edited by Edward S. Mason, p. 46. Cambridge, Mass.: Harvard University Press, 1960.

Rutledge, Wiley B. "Significant Trends in Modern Incorporation Statutes." 22 *Wash. U.L.Q*. 304 (1937).

Sabine, George H. *A History of Political Theory*. rev. ed. New York: Henry Holt & Co., 1951.

Scheiber, Harry. *The Ohio Canal Era: A Case Study of Government and the Economy, 1820–1861*. Athens, Ohio: Ohio University Press, 1969.

Schlatter, Richard. *Private Property: The History of an Idea*. New Brunswick, N.J.: Rutgers University Press, 1951.

Schumpeter, Joseph A.
   (1) "Economic Theory and Entrepreneurial History." In Harvard University Research Center in Entrepreneurial History, *Change and the Entrepreneur: Postulates and Pat-*

terns for Entrepreneurial History. Cambridge, Mass.: Harvard University Press, 1949.

(2) *History of Economic Analysis.* Edited by Elizabeth Boody Schumpeter. New York: Oxford University Press, 1954.

Scott, Austin Wakeman. *The Law of Trusts.* 3d ed. 6 vols. Boston: Little, Brown & Co., 1967.

Shaw, Edward S. Comment on Goldsmith, "Financial Structure and Economic Growth in Advanced Countries." In National Bureau of Economic Research, *Capital Formation and Economic Growth.* Princeton, N.J.: Princeton University Press, 1955.

Skilton, Robert H. "Field Warehousing as a Financing Device." 1961 *Wis. L. Rev.* 221.

Smith, Adam. *An Inquiry into the Nature and Causes of the Wealth of Nations.* 2 vols. London and New York: J. M. Dent & Sons, Ltd., 1930.

Smith, Henry Nash. *Virgin Land: The American West as Symbol and Myth.* Cambridge, Mass.: Harvard University Press, 1950.

Smith, Joseph H. *Cases and Materials on the Development of Legal Institutions.* St. Paul: West Publishing Co., 1965.

Smith, Walter B. *Economic Aspects of the Second Bank of the United States.* Cambridge, Mass.: Harvard University Press, 1953.

Sobel, Robert. *The Big Board: A History of the New York Stock Market.* New York: Free Press of Glencoe, Ill., 1965.

Stern, Robert L.

(1) "The Commerce Clause and the National Economy, 1933–1946." 59 *Harv. L. Rev.* 645, 883 (1946). Also in Association of American Law Schools, *Selected Essays on Constitutional Law,* 1938–1962, p. 218. St. Paul: West Publishing Co., 1963.

(2) "The Scope of the Phrase Interstate Commerce." 41 *A.B.A.J.* 823. Also in *Selected Essays, supra,* p. 298.

Stevens, Robert S.

(1) *Handbook on the Law of Private Corporations.* 2d ed. St. Paul: West Publishing Co., 1949.

(2) "Close Corporations and the New York Business Corporations Laws of 1961." 11 *Buffalo L. Rev.* 481 (1962).

Stiles, Ned B. See Baum and Stiles.

Stimson, Frederic J. *American Statute Law.* 2 vols. Boston: Boston Book Co., 1886, 1892.

Stocking, George W., and Myron W. Watkins. *Monopoly and Free Enterprise*. New York: Twentieth Century Fund, 1951.

Stryker, Perrin. *The Character of the Executive*. New York: Harper & Bros., Harper Torchbook, 1961.

Sutton, Francis X., and Seymour E. Harris, Carl Kaysen, and James Tobin. *The American Business Creed*. Cambridge, Mass.: Harvard University Press, 1956.

Thorelli, Hans B. *The Federal Antitrust Policy: Origination of an American Tradition*. Baltimore: Johns Hopkins Press, 1955.

Timberg, Sigmund. "Corporate Fictions." 46 *Colum. L. Rev.* 533 (1946).

Tobin, James. See Sutton, Harris, Kaysen, and Tobin.

Tunks, Lehan K. "Categorization and Federalism: 'Substance' and 'Procedure' after Erie Railroad v. Tompkins." 34 *Ill. L. Rev.* 271 (1939).

Turner, Donald F. See Kaysen and Turner.

von Mehren, Arthur, and John C. McCarroll. "The Proxy Rules: A Case Study in the Administrative Process." 29 *Law & Contemp. Prob.* 728 (1964).

Walden, Jerrold L. "More About *Noerr*: Lobbying, Antitrust and the Right to Petition." 14 *U.C.L.A. L. Rev.* 1211 (1967).

Warren, Charles
  (1) *The Making of the Constitution*. Boston: Little, Brown & Co., 1928.
  (2) *The Supreme Court in United States History*. rev. ed. 2 vols. Boston: Little, Brown & Co., 1935.

Watkins, Myron M. See Stocking and Watkins.

Weber, Max. *Max Weber on Law in Economy and Society*. Edited by Max Rheinstein. Cambridge, Mass.: Harvard University Press, 1954.

Whyte, William H., Jr. *The Organization Man*. New York: Simon & Schuster, 1956.

Wilburn, Jean Alexander. *Biddle's Bank: The Crucial Years*. New York: Columbia University Press, 1967.

Williams, Robin M., Jr. *American Society: A Sociological Interpretation*. New York: Alfred A. Knopf, 1951.

Williston, Samuel. "History of the Law of Business Corporations before 1800," 2 *Harv. L. Rev.* 105 (1888). Also in Association of American Law Schools, *Select Essays in Anglo-American Legal History*. 3 vols. 3:195. Boston: Little, Brown & Co., 1909.

Wohl, R. Richard. "Henry Noble Day: A Study in Good Works,

1808–1890." In *Men in Business,* edited by William Miller. Cambridge, Mass.: Harvard University Press, 1952.

Wright, Benjamin F. *The Contract Clause of the Constitution.* Cambridge, Mass.: Harvard University Press, 1938.

Zahler, Helene S. See Hacker and Zahler.

Page-Barbour Lecture Series

The Page-Barbour Lecture Foundation was founded in 1907 by a gift from Mrs. Thomas Nelson Page (née Barbour) and the Honorable Thomas Nelson Page for the purpose of bringing to the University of Virginia each session a series of lectures by an eminent person in some field of scholarly endeavor. The materials in this volume were presented by Professor Willard Hurst in April 1969, as the fifty-second series sponsored by the Foundation.

Index